A FOUCAULDIAN APPROACH TO INTERNATIONAL LAW

A Foucauldian Approach to International Law

Descriptive Thoughts for Normative Issues

LEONARD M. HAMMER
Senior Lecturer, Zefat College, Israel

ASHGATE

Published by
Ashgate Publishing Limited
Gower House
Croft Road
Aldershot
Hampshire GU11 3HR
England

Ashgate Publishing Company
Suite 420
101 Cherry Street
Burlington, VT 05401-4405
USA

Ashgate website: http://www.ashgate.com

British Library Cataloguing in Publication Data

Hammer, Leonard M.
A Foucauldian approach to international law : descriptive thoughts for normative issues
1. Foucault, Michel, 1926-1984 2. International law - Philosophy 3. Normativity (Ethics)
I. Title
341'.01

Library of Congress Cataloging-in-Publication Data
Hammer, Leonard M.
A Foucauldian approach to international law : descriptive thoughts for normative issues / by Leonard M. Hammer.
p. cm.
Includes bibliographical references and index.
ISBN-13: 978-0-7546-2356-4 (alk. paper) 1. International law. 2. Foucault, Michel, 1926-1984. I. Title.

KZ3410.H36 2007
341--dc22

2006031578

ISBN: 978-07546-2356-4

Printed and bound in Great Britain by TJ International Ltd, Padstow, Cornwall.

Contents

Acknowledgements *vii*

1 Introduction 1

2 Theoretical Grounds for International Law 7
Introduction 7
Some Approaches Thus Far 9
Additional Approaches 13
An Alternative Angle 17
Conclusion 27

3 Recognition, Transformation, and Power 29
Introduction 29
Recognition and State Perspective 31
Recognition and Process 33
Alternative Recognition 39
Conclusion 47

4 Transgressing Problems of Customary International Law 49
Introduction 49
What is Customary International Law? 51
Reference to Foucault 60
Conclusion 68

5 A Descriptive Moment for Freedom of Religion or Belief 71
Introduction 71
Considering the Human Right to Freedom of Religion or Belief 73
Individual Beliefs and Foucault 80
Implications for the Right to Freedom of Religion or Belief 91
Conclusion 95

6 Human Security from a Transformative Context 97
Introduction 97
Contrasting Human Security 99
Why Human Security 107
Human Security and an Alternative Approach 109
Conclusion 112

7 Non-Governmental Organizations and Power 115
Introduction 115
Global Civil Society Generally 117
Contending Issues and Problems 121
Reconsidering the Framework 124
Conclusion 128

8 Conclusion 129

Bibliography *135*
International Documents *135*
Judicial Decisions *136*
Books *136*
Articles *141*
Index *149*

Acknowledgements

A number of colleagues have been kind enough to have me present some of these chapters as lectures, presentations at conferences, or simply to discuss and reflect upon some of the ideas presented in the book. They include Reza Banakar, Marshall Breger, Eyal Chowers, Robert Destro, Gabriel Eckstein, Mathew Happold, Moshe Hirsh, Ruth Lapidoth, and Gabriel Wilner. I appreciate their time and efforts on my behalf.

As promised, I dedicate this book to Alon, Ronit, and Gidon, along with my unwitting muse, Sandy.

Chapter 1

Introduction

The purpose of this book is to offer alternative conceptions regarding the operation and potential role of international law within the international system. Via various notions proposed by Michel Foucault concerning our methodological modes of perception and the role of discourse formations, coupled with his approaches to power and knowledge, this book will shed light on inherent inconsistencies, and begin to propose some form of solutions, for a range of key topics within international law.

Referring to Foucault as a means of understanding and enhancing international law at first glance seems counterproductive. Foucault eschewed any notion of law or norms as maintaining an elevated position when compared to other forms of social forces and attendant developments. Further, he was involved in demonstrating methodologies that were de-coupled from a formalised legal system or normative order, maintaining (among other things) that analysis of these systems tended to ignore other external realities and the underlying processes that actually served as the driving force. An international system that tends to centralise the role of the sovereign state for example is problematic for Foucault, where the demand for a particular mode of analysis merits not only the incorporation of other actors, but also a wholly distinct form of scrutiny.

Recognising such an attitude towards law however need not lead to dismissing Foucault from consideration. Rather, it is important to remember that Foucault was not necessarily offering a theory as such, but rather analytic devices and forms of interpretation. Thus, one purpose in referring to Foucault throughout this work is to allude to his descriptive model as an avenue towards interpreting and further examining events and existing conceptions within the international system. The goal is to create a context for examination pursuant to Foucault's notions regarding social activity and forms of relations between the various actors.

Part of the difficulty with Foucault is that he provides questions, not answers, given that answers are reflective of merely temporary perceptions. Further, Foucault is linked to notions of disorder and resistance, preferring to consider the struggle and resistance surrounding interactions rather than actual (unattainable) solutions. Thus, referring to Foucault does not always imply an adoption of his ideas, but rather the means for initiating the development of a new line of thought, thereby addressing an at times chaotic international system beset by a host of influences and interests. The unique nature of Foucault is that one can grasp a number of disparate social developments and state concerns, and emerge with a context from which to initiate the advancement of an interpretation.

The proposal herein is to identify a framework that will not necessarily ameliorate all the various perceptions concerning international law, but begin to offer the means for grasping the surrounding changes and constantly shifting positions of the actors involved. International law is essentially stuck either within an outmoded statist approach, or an overly broad understanding of the significance of external actors like international organizations whose standing and influence are not altogether clear. Current interpretations of international law are rooted in a narrow attempt to demonstrate a functioning normative structure, deconstruct international law without offering a viable alternative, or interpret developments as reflective of an emerging and somewhat unwieldy ethical, legitimate, or constitutive (social) global order. The problem is that these approaches do not fully capture the essence of the changes and shifts to the international system nor allow for incorporation of different viewpoints and perspectives, especially when moving towards a relative or localised approach or shying away from a state-centric model. Additionally, it is interesting to consider that despite grand claims for a changed world with greater integration and broader representation, we are still beset by ethnic, religious, and national conflicts that limit the capacities for an improved international process and at times tend to create greater confusion within the desired normative order.

As Foucault operated within a particular ethos of inquiry, reference to his ideas can begin to extricate the international system from an overly systematic analysis, while at the same time maintain some of the underlying viability of an international normative order. Particularly, what is important is not the standards or elements of international law as definitive factors, but the manner by which the distinctions and associations are established within a system or political sphere. Thus, it is imperative to address the constant change and ongoing resistance of the international framework, a difficult task for any system that intends to impose some form of normative structure as a means of regulating the actors therein.

For Foucault, the state is a creation of our discourses and is not representative of a unified whole. Hence, power is coextensive with all forms of relationships, the state being merely one aspect of such power relationships given the possibility for influence of, as well as to be influenced by, the actions of others. Further, Foucault proposed notions of power and the relationship with knowledge that can assist the international subsystem of non-state actors in understanding surrounding events without necessarily abandoning the state and the international framework. Rather, in line with Foucault's descriptive approach, the goal is to consider a framework of understanding that would enhance the international system while at the same time allow for consideration of a variety of viewpoints. Thus, the book considers the engagement of the ongoing shifts and changes inherent in any politicised system as a means of discerning the contexts of operation. The goal herein is to allow for methods that would consider a broader context of operation from which to distil an understanding of what is transpiring and developing in international law.

Each of the book chapters addresses various aspects of international law from a Foucauldian perspective. The idea is to account for some of the fundamental problems within international law, with the view towards relying on Foucault's understanding of the structure of society and manner of interaction. The chapters then will assess and consider the underlying problems posed by each doctrine, and offer an alternative approach and treatment by which to consider the specific topic of the chapter.

Chapter 2 refers to international legal theory, considering a variety of viewpoints and approaches to international law, including recent assertions that have accounted for the incorporation of non-state actors as well. Moving away from an overly critical analysis, the chapter will offer Foucault's transgressive approach to overall social relations, including his understanding of the role of law and the state. Coupled with his perception of power and knowledge as forming an ongoing re-interpretation of the relevant relations, one emerges with an encapsulation of Foucault's basic notions that can assist an international system caught up in too narrow an understanding of power and the role of the state, and broaden the context of examination and operation. This chapter shall serve as the basis for understanding Foucault and the manner by which he will be referred to throughout the book.

The third chapter moves from theory to relations between states, particularly regarding the manner by which a state might acquire standing and personality within the international system via international recognition. Referring specifically to the recognition of states allows for an accounting of a doctrine that operates in a political context, despite attempts to accord it some form of normative status. A host of inadequately considered external considerations and influences also maintain relevancy for recognition. The proposal in Chapter 3 is to adhere to a process-oriented form of recognition, one that commingles notions of politics and policy with norms, with the process of recognition serving as the focus rather than the eventual outcome between the states. Acknowledging that recognition is essentially a matter of behavioural modulations (including political factors that drive forward a decision) as well as a reflection of relational power as understood by Foucault, one can emerge with a better understanding of recognition and the manner by which it can be referred to within the international system.

Chapter 4 addresses a key source of international law, that being customary international law. Custom as a source of law possesses a host of recurring fundamental problems, including the processes used to identify the norm, the weight accorded the principal elements of custom, and its actual application. Recognising that assertions pertaining to a customary norm derive from subjective interpretations generally pursuant to a state's unique interests, custom does not necessarily represent the truth of the assertion but is the result of the utilisation of emerging norms for use by the state. Customary norms are subject to ongoing change due not only to the subjective nature of the process, but also because external influences outside the purview of the sovereign state continuously force alterations to its composition and status. Hence it seems of greater beneficence to inquire *why* a particular claim regarding custom reflects the so-called 'truth' of the assertion at a given stage and *how* did one reach the point whereby an individual, state or international body can maintain grounds for making an assertion regarding the status of a customary norm.

Additionally, Chapter 4 will incorporate Foucault's understanding of discourse formations. Custom is not only a matter of ascertaining the amorphous notion of practice among the states, but also is a reflection of the social condition and historical development that serves to influence and change the actions of a state and other relevant actors. The 'discourse' that forms a part of custom incorporates a broad gamut of international and domestic actors, including the individual, non-governmental organisations, the state, and international bodies. Asserted thoughts are treated as objects in their own right, rather than examining the actual content of the thoughts, with a view towards ascertaining and understanding the process by which such assertions arose.

Moving away from the state and towards other international aspects, the remaining chapters shall examine more recent developments within the international system that implicitly rely on a broader notion of international law beyond the state. The issues to be examined incorporate other actors and internationally developed norms both from a top-down approach, such as international human rights as derived from treaties, as well as from a bottom-up perspective, such as the role of non-governmental organisations and the emergence of human security as a means for addressing some of the current problems in the world at large.

Starting with international human rights, Chapter 5 considers the role of human rights via reference to the right to freedom of religion or belief. Freedom of religion or belief is a fundamental right beset by problems of misapprehension and misapplication. Foucault is enlightening due to his approach towards social relationships and development of human ideas, such that all entities exercising power or espousing a human right are part of a broader framework of social relations. Thus, the power of a human right norm is not only that it represents a right per se, but also that it serves as a form of producing individual and social reactions and furthering the continuing social discourse. Particularly concerning the human right to freedom of religion or belief, it is important to account for the social dimensions that the right entails. Foucault's approach to power then can assist not only with positioning human rights within the international system, but also to integrate an atomist oriented human rights system into the broader social discourse.

Chapter 6 turns towards the notion of human security, a relatively recent and still emerging concept that has been touted as an important inroad into addressing a variety of concerns within the international system. Specifically, human security has been identified for addressing problems of less-developed states and the means by which to correct their ills, as well as various normative lacunae within international law that has been difficult to incorporate changed circumstances, such as within the humanitarian law context. The problem has been one of context, especially how to conform notions of human security into the international system. Human security however serves a process-oriented function, focusing on local necessities and recognising the role of a variety of actors according to their specific needs. Such an approach involves the conceptualisation of an operative method without necessarily being linked to a strict normative framework. Thus, Foucault's attitude to norms and his understanding of power provides a strong contextual framework for the actual operation and implementation of human security notions. Foucault recognises the capacity for a process-oriented context, without being weighed down by a normative framework.

Chapter 7 engages newer paradigms within international law and the manner by which they can assist the international system. Part of the problem with the liberalist approach has been a lack of critique, an almost complacent acceptance of the market oriented approach via a sound rule of law as the sole means towards peace and stability. Turning specifically to global civil society and non-governmental organisations, the goal of the chapter is to account for what has been understood as new directions within the international framework. Recognising in particular the variety of problems associated with non-governmental organisations, especially internal and external accountability issues, the chapter will offer the means for engaging an approach to international relations and international law that incorporates various non-state entities as viable actors. In particular, Foucault's understanding of power is quite apt here and assists the international system in according an active role to the variety of players in the global civil society framework.

The concluding chapter offers additional suggestions for further study via the approach of Foucault. It is hoped that the book can serve as a starting point from which to consider other aspects that have emerged within the international system that can be better understood, leading to better applications, via a Foucauldian perspective. As noted at the outset, the goal is not to critically de-construct the international system, but to explicate emerging concepts that have served to alter the underlying structure of international law and international relations especially given the emergence of new actors and concepts, such as to allow for a better overall functioning system that properly addresses the needs of all actors participating therein.

Chapter 2

Theoretical Grounds for International Law

Introduction

Public international law is beset by issues questioning its legitimacy, viability and at times the very existence of such law.[1] Even for those in the

1 For recent overviews of approaches to international law, or at least representative examples of some of the different perspectives that have been asserted, see Kingsbury, B. (2005), 'The International Legal Order', *IILJ Working Paper 2003/1* (History and Theory of International Law Series) available at: www.iilj.org (relying on Grotius as a means to combine both the source and content of the rules); Rajagopal, B. (2003), *International Law from Below: Development, Social Movements and Third World Resistance* (Cambridge University Press, UK) (social movements as a better reflection of international law and its development); Raustiala, K. (2002), 'The Architecture of International Cooperation: Transgovernmental Networks and the Future of International Law', 43 *Va. J. Intl. L.* 1 (transgovernmental networks as a means of entrenching international cooperation and liberal internationalism); Guzman, A. (2002), 'A Compliance-Based Theory of International Law', 90 *Calif. L. Rev.* 1823 (compliance as reflected by rational, self-interested, states); Stark, B. (2002), 'After/word(s): "Violations of Human Dignity" and Postmodern International Law', 27 *Yale J. Intl. L.* 315 (embracing the fragmented nature of public international law); Kennedy, D. (2000), 'When Renewal Repeats: Thinking Against the Box', 32 *N. Y. U. J. Intl. L. and Pol.* 335 ; Simpson, G. (2000), 'The Situation on the International Legal Theory Front: The Power of Rules and the Rule of Power', 11 *E. J. Intl. L.* 439–465 (critiquing Byers, M. (1999), *Custom, Power and the Power of Rules* (Oxford University Press, UK) and offering an overview of different approaches within international law and international relations); Georgiev, D. (1993), 'Politics or Rule of Law: Deconstruction and Legitimacy in International Law', 4 *E. J. Intl. L.* 1–14 (referring to legitimacy as a means of grounding international law); Allot, P. (1992), 'Reconstituting Humanity – New International Law', 3 *E. J Intl. L.* 219–252 (a cosmopolitan approach, asserting that law can actualize social objectives); Carty (1991), 'Critical International Law Recent Trends in the Theory of International Law', 2 *E. J. Intl. L.* 66–96 (adopting deconstructionist approach, with goal of understanding allegations of states in terms of cultural pre-suppositions); Koskenniemi, M. (1989), *From Apology to Utopia: The Structure of*

international law field who recognize some form of consensual structure or agreements between states, the issue of deeming international law as 'law' constantly lingers in the background. Notions of a universal system are too easily dismissed due to instances where states have acted contrary to a norm, assertions of relativism in the application of the law, or cries of neo-colonialism deriving from a favoured leaning towards a Western orientation within the international system. Similarly, consensus has been too easily undermined by the will of hegemonic states or political influencing within the confines of international organizations that stymies the emergence of an international legal order.

Within the context of international relations, international law has been caught between realist assertions of state interests as superseding international law, institutionalists that accord some form of role for international legal making organizations, or cosmopolitan assumptions of moral state behaviour with a view towards the identification of an existing social order. Each approach is of course beset with inherent problems, whereby examples of state behaviour can be demonstrated to either prove or disprove the asserted position. Thus, while international organizations might actually serve to entrench international law or have some form of norm-creating role, enough examples exist of states in the breach, or counter-examples where an organization acted contrarily in a similar situation, to call into question the notion of international law as law.

It seems that attempts at discerning the underlying drive of international law has moved beyond the notion of universality or consensus, to one of unearthing the differences between the players and treating inherent conflicts as the reality. Alternatively, many have jumped on the realist bandwagon, asserting that international law does not exist as such, acting as a tool of the state and merely standing as a reflection of particular interests. Less extreme realist views contend that while not wholly normative, international law might reflect some form of underlying understanding between states, recognizing that the application will be subject to the relevant whims or interests of the state.

What have been difficult to consider are attempts to transgress this seemingly dichotomous battle, be it between a critical and positivist or consensualist approach, or between a universalist or cosmopolitan view and a realist position. International law too easily succumbs to a deconstructionist position or folds to realist assertions regarding the actual

---

International Legal Argument (Finnish Lawyers Pub. Comp., Helsinki) (critiquing key approaches within international law, as discussed *infra*).

behaviour of states. Acknowledging that state discourse is latent with political interests and inherent values makes it quite difficult to emerge with a standard when accounting for the key sources of international law that heavily rely on such discourse.[2]

Part of the underlying problem has been considering a framework for changes that have developed within international law over the past century given the growth of international and regional organisations, a move towards globalisation with its attendant local and international effects (economic and social), and the rise in influence by actors external to the state. The assertion herein, and throughout the rest of the book, is that an alternative approach as dictated by the theories of Michel Foucault can begin to address some of the problems. The proposal centres on a framework that allows for inherent contradictions, given what can be called a transformative understanding of the international system and a transgressive approach to one's perception of international society. The advantage in referring to Foucault is the possibility to ameliorate contrasting viewpoints by addressing the underlying changes to the system. A clearer image of present day international law and the role of such law in the international framework can be better elucidated.

Following a brief overview of some of the proposed approaches to international law, this chapter shall offer a methodology to international law considering it from a descriptive standpoint given an alternative understanding of power and its link with knowledge, which will serve as a blueprint for analysis of the specific issues in the ensuing chapters.

Some Approaches Thus Far

The problems identified with international law have centred on the ambiguity of the process, given the link between international law and political (along with legal) processes. Even more profoundly than in domestic jurisdictions, where laws also result from a political process, the international system is problematic because there is no actual 'legal' system; the states are creating the law for their own regulation. Thus, unlike in domestic jurisdictions, enforcement aspects are lacking or are weak to the point that the existence of some form of legal system per se does not adequately exist.

---

2 *See* discussion *infra* at Chapter 4.

This lack of a viable framework comparable to a domestic one is rather frustrating for legally trained individuals. The infusion of inherently contrasting state interests among the states leads to ambiguities in the variety of documents and treaties that serve as sources for international law. This usually is because such sources of law result from high-end political negotiations where the goal is to protect and preserve the state and its interests rather than solely create a viable and enforceable legal norm.

Indeed, in attempting to address this problem of international law's open-ended nature, some have concluded that international law is inherently ambiguous.[3] Following from this, international law is accused of being a fragmented process and structure,[4] with little notion of state accountability, thereby making any attempt at assessment a difficult exercise. International lawyers are left to either assert their position pursuant to their pre-determined interests or those of the state, or to acknowledge the inherent problems and attempt to construct some form of viable ongoing system that recognises international law.

Additionally, the lack of a network leads to inherent inconsistencies within international law. That is, the law as such might derive from a particular definitive source, like a treaty, but the state will pull the particular norm or edict towards its own direction and towards a particular meaning that best serves its interests. This of course brings to bear the issues surrounding the place of international law and its role, if at all, in the regulation of states and their actions.

International legal theories have proposed a number of approaches by way of explaining what is happening within the international system. For example, Koskenniemi places the framework of the issue within the context of normative versus consensual endpoints.[5] A normative approach recognises international law as operating to create specific norms that are binding on the state. It is an attempt to identify an objective application of international law to all the relevant actors (principally the states).

The attempt to objectify international law is problematic given the political aspects that are implied by the system. Because international law is founded on the notion of the will of states, the latter will tend to cancel out any form of objectivity. Either international law is too political

3 Stark (2002); Carty (1991).
4 Stark (2002).
5 Koskenniemi (1989).

given the reference to state's will and its capacity to assert power, or international law is unrealistic given the tie to utopian ideals of normative objectivity.[6] In essence, the claim is that international law would be hard pressed to exist without some form of concreteness based on state's will – at least as a means of providing a social context. Presumably, a consensus derives from the overall understanding of the various states involved. At the same time however international law also must have some aspect of objective normativity to allow for effective operation and application. Yet, combining the two (concrete state will and objective normativity) proves to be rather difficult given their pull in seemingly opposite directions.

Other attempts to identify the basis for international law have proposed some form of dichotomous distinction. Thus, Kennedy frames the issue within the context of the natural law approach and the imposition of some form of objective standards, as opposed to a positivist understanding of law dictated by the states.[7] Objective standards are linked to the so-called natural law of states, thereby preventing anarchy and preserving some form of state-to-state relations. A positivist understanding is looking more at the interests of states and the actual means by which the process is carried out in a practical, more realist, manner.

The former of course begs the question regarding objectivity, associated with many of the challenges to the natural law approach regarding its creation and identification. The problem is further heightened upon factoring in non-Western states and relative approaches to law based on religion, culture, or other epistemological differences. The latter positivist approach raises the issue of consent among states and whether that is an attainable outcome.

Kennedy frames the distinction as one of sovereign equality (objectivity) as opposed to acknowledging sovereign authority. States are either independent and acting without any overarching authority, or are linked to notions of sovereign equality with the proper application of international law when appropriate. Thus, one is stuck between doctrines of law versus the actual practice of law, similar to Koskenniemi's linking the issue to concreteness (based on practice) versus normativity (based on doctrine).

---

6 *See also* Koskenniemi, M. (1990) 'The Politics of International Law', 1 *E. J. Intl. L.* 4–32.

7 For an outline of Kennedy's ideas (and more), see Kennedy, D. (2000), 'When Renewal Repeats: Thinking Against the Box', 32 N. Y. U. J. Intl. L. and Pol. 335.

It is interesting to contrast various approaches proposed by international relations scholars whose frameworks have at times been adopted by those in the international law field. The division similarly perceives the role of international law as either those of the realists, where international law is merely a reflection of state interests, as opposed to the cosmopolitan or institutionalist camps who ascribe some form of regulatory role to international law or attempt to impose a value-laden system of consent. Regime theorists for example understand international law as playing a role in establishing order between states and international organisations while institutionalists incorporate notions of normativity within the law, recognizing the imposition of some form of objective standard on a state. Recent international legal literature has recognized for example the importance of social policies and various other forces that affect state actions in a more nuanced manner,[8] as well as the advent of globalisation that has moved the international framework away from a state-centric orientation.[9]

The realists link to state interests is in essence similar to the international law approach of law as having only a causal role resulting from practice. An amelioration of this realist framework can be found in a recent book by Goldsmith and Posner where the authors interpret international law as a reflection of state interests, such that the authors consider international law as instrumental rational choices taken by states to further their power and welfare.[10]

Thus, there exists an inherent tension between different approaches to international law that depends upon the desired interpretation one may give to state relations, or to the creation of a legal framework meant to regulate the actions of states.

Of course, there are positions in between these extremes where commentators attempt to propose methods of combining between the

---

8 Berman, P. (2006), 'Seeing Beyond the Limits of International Law', 84 *Tex. L. R.* 1265 (given multiple affiliations within and without the state influencing state policy, the overall vision of the international community is not solely a unitary state choice regarding rational choice, but must account for the variety of voices within an enlarged international framework).

9 *See* e.g. Garcia F. (2005), 'Globalization and the Theory of International Law', B.C. Law School Faculty Papers, paper #93, available at: http://lsr.nellco.org/bc/bclsfp/papers/93.

10 Goldsmith, J. and Posner, E. (2005), *The Limits of International Law* (Oxford University Press, NY).

objective/normative and the consensual/positive aspects. For example, there are attempts to bridge the gap of normative objectivity and notions of state interests via the role of legitimacy.[11] That is a legitimate assertion of an objective norm can occur where there is consent among states that proper procedures have been adhered to in creating and enforcing the norm. The concrete aspect is met given adherence to necessary and valid procedures, and the objective factor is upheld given the identification of a specific norm. Thus, law is distinguished from politics where agreed to procedures are followed which reflect accepted social behaviour (concreteness) and that bring to the fore a state obligation (normative objectivity).[12]

The problem with such an approach is that it does not remove the value-laden notions inherent in the objective, normative, side because it is clear that the definition or identification of such a norm is inherently linked to the values and interpretations of each state party. One might identify legitimacy via external factors such as the concreteness of a norm, however attaining some form of broader or universal understanding regarding the status or existence of a norm will doubtless be subject to ongoing debate and at the mercy of the subjective interests of the entity making the assertion.

Similarly, the notion of a legitimate form of consent-creating procedure will be inherently linked to a specific understanding or perception of each state, usually depending on their interests at stake or their policy and political goals. It seems that legitimacy theory as grounds for state action becomes a result-oriented process that removes attention from the actual techniques and tactics used by the state to achieve the result.[13] Any sense of amelioration does not address the problems with international law, but actually seems to heighten them.

Additional Approaches

One of the key methods for considering international law and its potential link to other disciplines, in particular international relations, has been the emergence of sociological models of international law. The focus has been a strive to combine realism and the importance of state interests with some

11 The turn to legitimacy generally relies on the work of Frank, T. (1990), *The Power of Legitimacy Among Nations* (Oxford University Press, UK).

12 *See* e.g. Georgiev (1993).

13 Hunt, A. and Wickham G. (1994), *Foucault and Law: Towards a Sociology of Law as Governance* (Pluto Press, London) at 16–17.

form of cosmopolitan or consensual understanding of international law that recognizes the co-existence of both aspects in a structured manner, thereby developing a sound normative system of international law.

An important approach to international law has been an inter-disciplinary consideration, turning specifically to international relations as a source of inspiration and explication. By way of example, Byers has been a strong proponent of integrating international relations with international law to achieve some form of consensual standard.[14] Essentially, Byers proposes an accounting for the collective notions of states based on their consensus of what is legally relevant. This is an important inroad into expanding international law to incorporate important factors that influence and even determine the normative elements of the law. It also acknowledges some form of independent causal role for international law, beyond the confines of a realist interpretation, by attempting to identify the factors that go into the composition of law and its creation of some form of international social order

A similar approach is noted by a compliance-based theory of international law.[15] The basic notion of a compliance system, again referring to the international relations model, is that because states act in a self-interested manner, there are instances where they will comply with international law when it is beneficial to do so.[16]

The problems identified with these approaches are similar to the aforementioned issues regarding legitimacy doctrine. That is, in a practical sense, how is one to assess the legal relevance of a collective belief? Further, how is one to even identify some form of consensus let alone legitimise such a consensus?[17] The notion of legitimizing an emerging consensus does not remove the inherent values (or interests) of states that have formed the crux of the realist critique. Indeed, one can assert that referring to collective notions of states based on consensus entrenches Western oriented approaches, providing a platform for the more powerful states and removing the objective, normative, content that is being sought.

---

14 Byers (1999).

15 Guzman (2002).

16 Guzman (2002) elaborates on the compliance theory by demonstrating how it is more conducive to developing viable customary international law, rather than relying on the traditional elements that do not capture the essence of state interests.

17 *See* e.g. Simpson (2000).

Taking the analysis a step further have been proposals centring on sociological models of sovereignty. While the state as a realist entity is pursuing its interests, there also are social norms that serve a constructive function, especially influential on states when accounting for important social institutions. Thus, the argument goes, states are not the sole determinants of their construct, but also result from global cultural models via cultural processes that are organized at the global level.

The central focus in this constructive approach is the effects of institutions such as international organisations on states.[18] International law develops due to the isomorphic nature of the state, an entity that has been shaped by cultural processes, such that states will combine to promote globally legitimate goals, like human rights or protecting the environment.[19]

In a sense this understanding mirrors the proposal enunciated by Carty that states are linked by a competing community paradigm, whereby there is no final or determinative answer as such to the issue of international law and its identification; rather the occasional normative solutions are to be bridged by an understanding of the cultural pre-suppositions of the actors.[20] The notion of looking at global cultural models furthers an understanding of the cultural suppositions, thereby entrenching a better understanding of the process and possible outcome for international law

The proposed model however seems to shy away from the inherent tensions that exist within the international framework. That is, even if states are commendably promoting globally legitimate goals, such as upholding protection for the environment, it is still the states that are violating these obligations. The proposal does not go far enough in examining the significance of this global to state relationship as a means of defining international law nor in addressing the underlying meaning of a cultural construct outside of a Western-oriented model. The tension of normative objectivity versus consensual understanding of international law still exists, even with a broader explanation that refers to cultural presuppositions.

18 *See* e.g. Goodman, R. and Jenks, D. (2003), 'Towards an Institutional Theory of Sovereignty', 55 *Stan. L. Rev.* 1749.

19 *See also* Allot (1992), noting that the goal of law within society is to actualize the underlying social objectives that define a society.

20 Carty (1991).

Another approach, albeit somewhat mirroring notions of managerialism within the international relations context, has been to examine transgovernmental networks as part of the international law process.[21] The understanding is that the state exists in a disaggregated form due to greater interactions and economic reliance between states. Coupled with a seemingly better form of treaty compliance, one achieves a sounder form of international law. Similar to the compliance theory where rational self-interested states will be inclined to uphold international law, the understanding is that the emergence of actors other than states will serve to entrench international norms in state-state relations. The call for better treaty compliance for example is understood to provide the normative basis for upholding the international norms that are developing.

This approach is interesting in that it begins to recognize actors other than states as applying a functional and formative role in the international process.[22] What is emerging from such views is the notion that states are not the central or even dominant player in international law given the inherent influences that derive from globalisation, forcing the state to look beyond its self to determine norms and assess its actions.

Another key benefit of the aforementioned proposal is that it reflects an understanding of international law that allows for the development of a system in constant flux. The inherent tension within international law where some form of normative standard is sought for a system beset by issues of consent and state interests can begin to be understood and addressed.

Nonetheless, the approach is still rooted within the basic dichotomy that haunts international law – that being the normative objective notion, presumably being derived from treaties that have stronger compliance, and the issue of state interests, that being reliance on organizations that essentially mirror a Western orientation or are constantly subject to the whims of hegemonic states given the overlying context of *realpolitik*. What we are left with are various attempts to either ameliorate the two contrasting notions, or explanations regarding why one aspect, like transgovernmentalism, will be addressed by the other, such as stronger treaty compliance. Yet we are still trapped within the dichotomous circle,

---

21 Raustiala, K. (2002), 'The Architecture of International Cooperation Transgovernmental Networks and the Future of International Law', 43 *Va. J. Intl. L.* 1.

22 Hobe, S. (2002), 'The Era of Globalisation as a Challenge to International Law', 40 *Duq. L. Rev.* 655.

thereby making it difficult to move beyond the problem. Visions of neo-realism, based on distinctions of material power raise the question of why do we have norms at all? Neo-liberalism, on the other hand, which is linked to notions of cooperation and consensus, raises the question of how do norms operate outside of a cooperative context?[23] Similarly for the deconstructionist school, one is still left within a context of doubt, or at the very least within an ongoing state of conflict that does not fully address the notion of obligations implied by norms. Thus, concluding for example that there exist occasional instances of conciliation does not seem to offer a sufficient solution or a better understanding of international law.

An Alternative Angle

The major issues that seem to derive from the variety of analyses of international law centre on its ambiguity and how to integrate a normative context into a system that seemingly shuns such an approach, as well as how to address the advent of external actors that have risen to the fore in international law. Granted the state still maintains centre stage, yet how may one adequately incorporate other significant actors, such as international organisations, individuals, non-governmental organisations or other social movements into the existing normative context of international law? The proposals noted do allow some form of external participation outside of the state, yet do not fully address the manner by which such actors are part of the process in a way that allows for further development and growth of the international system.

The key factor that will be developed herein is the notion of transgressing the current international structure to incorporate all relevant actors, as well as offering what can be termed a transformative view of international law pursuant to Foucault's understanding of power. It is asserted that such an approach can begin to address the dichotomous issue of norms/objectivity and state interests by transgressing the context of examination. Furthermore, an alternative notion of power will begin to address the manner by which states alter their positions, thereby recognizing the proper role of external actors as well.

A similar approach has been proposed by Rajagopal via a focus on the importance of social movements[24] and it merits consideration.

---

23 Thomas, W. (2001), *The Ethics of Destruction: Norms and Force in International Relations* (Cornell University Press, NY).

24 Rajagopal (2003). *See also* Rajagopal, B. (2003), 'International Law and Social Movements: Challenges of Theorizing Resistance', 41 *Colum. J. Transnatl. L.* 397.

The contention is that the international process is moving away from a state-oriented model, especially when considering that the state is not necessarily the centre of power. Rather, for Rajagopal, the focus shifts to social movements and notions of resistance, and not concepts of governance centred on state control. The key factors are a move away from institutionalism with the state as a central player and a focus on private political power and the manner in which social movements (not solely linked to formal non-governmental organisations) play a role to shape international law. Thus far, institutions, including states, have leaned towards an individual oriented structure pursuant to liberal theory, an inclination that has caused on over-reliance on democratic political systems as grounds for action and legitimacy, albeit at times a rather undemocratic form of practice in actuality.[25] The public/private distinction within liberal oriented institutions also are fading away as external actors play a more active role and private actors fill in a variety of governmental functions via greater privatisation.

From a power standpoint, the sovereign will is not the only venue for exercising power nor are the variety of institutions that have been established. Rather, social actors are quite heterogeneous, reaching the outer limits of the social structure, such as to indicate a variety of power venues beyond the confines of formalised institutions or the state and an enlarged focus on localised entities. Given the concentration on actual practice rather then formalised institutions, the key issue for Rajagopal is how to envisage the manner of relationships between the variety of actors involved in the process? For Rajagopal, the key is localised social movements as an inroad to understanding.

Following on from the aforementioned analysis, referring to Foucault will assist in perceiving an alternative structure within the international framework. Foucault's understanding of governmentality and the relation between social movements or individuals and the state or other institutions was transgressive. The state was not the central actor in the relationship but rather part of a matrix of power assertions that allows for the incorporation of a variety of actors and their contributions to the development of international law.[26] Examining the state does not necessarily demand an examination of its military or economic power, but rather how the state is articulated into the activities of the government and its relations with

25 Rajagopal (2003) at 138.

26 Amoore, L. and Langley, P. (2005), 'Global civil society and global governmentality', in Germain, R. and Kenny, M. (eds), *The Idea of Global Civil Society: Politics and ethics in a globalizing era* (Routledge, UK) at 147.

other actors. What is important is not to discern what is, but rather, from a methodological standpoint, how power is being used and what effects are produced as a result.

The transgressive notion is relevant for understanding international law given an emergence of multiple sites for addressing social and political issues external to the formalised state framework, such as to suggest that the state is not maintaining full and complete control.[27] What begs attention then is not the state as the central actor, but an understanding of the variety of actors' use of techniques and tactics of domination to understand the framework and forms of relations.[28]

What distinguishes Foucault is that he understood power and its application as being subject to constant change and alteration. The legally derived power of the ruling authority or of the sovereign entity as the case may be, is rather fragile. There exist a host of influences that derive from a diverse array of actors external to the state and its apparatus that might be using their notion of power for their benefit. Power is an ongoing development that, because it is ever changing, alters the context for examination. Given the multiplicity of actors that assert power or that maintain the capacity to do so, the real examination is the complex interplay of social relations between the various actors.[29] Hence deeming the state as the sovereign creator of law is an exaggeration of sorts due to the variety of influences and external developments that go into the development of laws.[30] State sovereignty undergoes constant changes and shifts to emerge more as a social product resulting from discourse and knowledge, rather than existing as a defined territorial entity.[31] This is particularly the case for

---

27 Rose, N. and Miller, P. (1992), 'Political Power Beyond the State: problematics of government', 43 *Brit. J. Soc.* 173–206.

28 *See* e.g. Hunt, A. (1992), 'Foucault's Expulsion of Law: Toward a Retrieval', 17 *Law and Soc. Inquiry* 1–38 (critiquing Foucault's approach to domestic law); Allen, B. (1998), 'Foucault and Modern Political Philosophy', 164–198 in Moss, J. (ed.) *The Later Foucault: Politics and Philosophy* (Sage Pub. London).

29 Ivison, D. (1998), 'The Disciplinary Moment: Foucault, Law, and the Reinscription of Rights', in Mass, J. (ed.) The Later Foucault (Sage Publications, UK).

30 Wickham, G. (2002), 'Foucault and Law', 248–266 in Banakar, R. and Travers, M. (eds), *An Introduction to Law and Social Theory* (Hart Pub. Oxford); Constable, M. (1991), 'Foucault and Walzer: Sovereignty, Strategy, and the State', 24 *Polity* 269.

31 Smith, S. (2001), 'Globalization and the Governance of Space: a critique of Krasner on Sovereignty', 1 *Intl. Rel. of the Asia Pacific* 199 (noting in particular the effect of globalization on state operations).

the international system as it presently stands, when factoring in external influences such as international organisations and non-governmental organisations along with a variety of political influences, to name but a few. The various social agents disperse power, leading to a fragmented political field that is constituted by a variety of social identities.[32]

Thus, upon considering the law and Foucault, one is immediately confronted with the notion that gauging the influence of the law is not solely a matter of sovereign command or actual force by the state, but is more precisely one of resistance among the variety of social forces.[33] Law is not a final result from which emanates decisions or directives, but rather is part of the social power system. While law provides some form of framework for action, and law, like other social influences, assists in constituting disciplinary power, it does not sit above the disciplinary power. The law then like other social phenomenon or influence is not solely a preventive mechanism but maintains some form of creative and productive aspect[34] meriting an examination of the disciplinary role of law and the imposition of such discipline by the ruling authority. In the words of Foucault:

> ...instead of privileging law as a manifestation of power, it would be better to try and identify the different techniques of constraint that it brings into play.[35]

Law is not unique because of the capacity to control, but rather due to the manner in which such control is attempted and the significance of such an attempt on our social relationships. Even within the context of rights where greater governmental involvement and regulation is demanded, the increased reference to protective laws need not be understood as preventive, but rather as acknowledging the role of individuals or other non-state groups (such as indigenous peoples) and their specific capacities that must be addressed, bringing into play their role regarding the use of power.[36]

---

32 Newman, S. (2004), 'The Place of Power in Political Discourse', 25 *Intl. Pol. Science Rev.* 139 (noting that while identities are displaced, the system also constitutes identity by recognising the inherent limits).

33 Baxter, H. (1996), 'Bringing Foucault into Law and Law into Foucault', 48 *Stanford Law Review* 449 at 453.

34 Tadros, V.(1998), 'Between Governance and Discipline: The Law and Michel Foucault', 18 *Oxford Journal of Legal Studies* 75 at 77–78.

35 Foucault, M. (1997), 'Society Must Be Defended', in Rabinow, P. (ed.) *Michel Foucault, Ethic: Essential works of Foucault 1954–1984, Volume 1* (The New Press, USA) at 59.

36 *See* discussion *infra* at Chapter 5.

The importance of perceiving what is normally understood to be a restrictive mechanism, i.e., law as limiting one's actions, as a productive one is that a legislature actually is acknowledging the role of a variety of social forces. A host of social influences are components in maintaining some form of influence within society. Similar to a variety of other social interactions, the disciplinary nature of the law itself does not singularly control individuals but produces particular subjects and in turn is the result of these particular subjects. That is, the law maintains some form of influence but that influence is part of a broader framework relating to the interaction of individuals and other actors, and the manner in which they might assert their influence.

The law does not serve a regulatory role between the state and the individual, but rather functions as part of the process in shaping individuals and allowing for their reactions that in turn further serve to shape and influence the social process. The law however does not sit above such a process but tends to be part of the ongoing change and assertions that individuals might adopt.

Within the international context, the role of law tends even more so towards a process-orientation rather than a regulatory role, especially as the variety of influences and lack of enforcement methods indicates a different role for international law that is not wholly comparable to a domestic system. For Foucault, governmentality moves beyond the sovereign state to encompass relations that order society pursuant to the discursive formations that create effects of truth within specific fields. The notion of discourse is an important factor for the international framework since the discourse is not founded as deriving from the subject given that the subject adopts a number of roles within a discursive field. What is important is the relation that is involved between the statements or assertions being made, moving the examination towards how the statement effects (or has effected) our perceptions. Thus, the permanence of the idea is not the issue, but rather the emergence and transformation of the statement itself is what merits examination.[37] It is important to identify the variety of elements

37 Foucault, M. (1969, trans. 1972), *The Archaeology of Knowledge* (Routledge, UK) at Chapter 2. In the words of Foucault, what is necessary is: 'to analyze the discourses themselves, that is, these discursive practices that are intermediary between words and things....These are the rules put into operation through a discursive practice at a given moment that explain why a certain thing is seen (or omitted); why it is envisaged under such an aspect and analyzed at such a level; why such a word is employed with such a meaning and in such a sentence. Consequently, the analysis starting from things and the analysis starting

within a discursive formation to discern the positions of the subjects and their derivations. That is why knowledge as derived from discourse is based in essence on ever-changing pre-suppositions that are constantly being challenged and displaced given the modification of positions following the incorporation of new forms of knowledge and understanding.

Additional thematic influences also exist within discourse, including political influences and external perceptions that provide structure for the discourse itself. Thus, the discourse creates a material effect beyond mere practice, as it captures the economic, social, and political positions and determinations to account for the various techniques that are being employed, and thereby lead to a proper delineation of the positions of the actors.[38] Discourse then does not create coherence as such, but rather allows for the study of divisions via discursive formations, where one can begin to identify a regularity or a correlation. Specifically within the international context, there are a host of actors and influences that secure institutional arrangements outside of the state context and that play a significant role in the formation of discourse that enter the arena of ideas and influences.[39]

Concomitant with an alternative understanding of law, one also must account for the form of relationships being developed between the variety of actors. Particularly, state power is not a conscious decision deriving from a state's exercise of sovereignty to assert a state's so called will. The latter is too diffuse a concept and is subject to a host of influences. Rather, power can be better understood as a transgressive notion that is external to a conscious decision given the role that all individuals maintain in creating such a reality. The contribution of Foucault lies in the realisation that power is not simply a relationship between entities, for example as between the individual and the state, nor is it a matter of dividing up power between various entities, such as between international organisations and the state. Rather, power is distributed throughout complex social actions which serve to modify the actions of others, and not because a dominant

---

from words appear at this moment as secondary in relation to prior analysis, which would be the discursive analysis.' Foucault, M. (1989), 'Foucault Live (Interviews, 1966–84)', Lotringer, S. (ed.) *(Semiotext(e)*, NY) at 51–52.

38 *See* e.g. Simons, J. (1995), *Foucault and the Political* (Routledge, UK) at 56.

39 Merlingen, M. (2003), 'Governmentality: Towards a Foucauldian Framework for the Study of International Governmental Organizations', 38 *Cooperation and Conflict* 361.

agent possesses power in any structured sense.[40] As a result, in the words of Foucault:

> One cannot confine oneself to analysing the state apparatus alone if one wants to grasp the mechanisms of power in their detail and complexity...I do not mean in any way to minimise the importance of effectiveness of State power. I simply feel that excessive insistence on its playing an exclusive role leads to the risk of overlooking all the mechanisms and effects of power which don't pass directly via the State apparatus, yet often sustain the State more effectively than its own institutions, enlarging and maximising its effectiveness.[41]

What develops then when considering the role of power, especially in the course of international law and relations, is that power is not a unit unto itself that develops following a variety of state assertions, but is recognised as a subjective notion given its source as deriving from an external plane.

While unstable in the micro level, power is a constant factor that circulates throughout all social relations.[42] In a sense, the actions of peripheral social agents serve to create alterations and indicate shifts in the so-called sovereign power's actions and directions. The existence of power as understood by Foucault is a series of multiple points of resistance[43] that serve to assist in identifying power. Because power is a multiple layered process, whereby many individuals or bodies will attempt to exercise their power, the assertion of such power becomes part of an ongoing process of domination and resistance.[44] One can maintain that power relations are

---

40 Rouse J. (1994), 'Power/Knowledge', 92–114 in Gutting, G. (ed.) *The Cambridge Companion to Foucault* (Cambridge University Press, USA) at 106.

41 Foucault, M. (1980), *Power/Knowledge: Selected Interviews and Other Writings 1972–1977* (Harvester Press, Sussex) at 72–73.

42 Lynch, R. (1998), 'Is Power All There Is? Michel Foucault and the "Omnipresence" of Power Relations', 42 *Philosophy Today* 65–70.

43 Foucault played on Clausewitz in noting that pursuant to our current world structure, politics is the continuation of war.

44 In a sense, this can address Lukes' problem with Foucault's approach to power. Lukes' key contention is that Foucault failed to account for the manner by which one is to secure compliance, such that if power is an ongoing development, what about instances of success or failure for a power relation as well as the means for identifying the subject? Lukes, S. (2005), *Power: A Radical View* (Palgrave Macmillan, NY, 2nd ed.) at 90–95. Referring to Foucault's transgressive approach towards social relations puts forward an alternative notion that recognizes an ongoing form of discourse subject to constant change and alteration, whereby instances of resistance or the failure of power form part of this discourse, representing the manner by which one forms and asserts power in social relations.

immanent in the social spaces occupied by the variety of actors. Power is a relational aspect as it depends on a multiplicity of targets and influences.

Additionally, it is important to note, upon considering the role of power as a source of delimitation, that power is not only influenced by social forces coming to the fore, but also of course influences social forces. Power is part of an ongoing and ever-changing relationship of resistance to the assertion of power. While influencing other actors, the actor asserting power also will be subject to influences and thus changes in the understanding of power accorded to the actor. Resistance to the assertions of power are not exterior to the power process but form an important role not only in creating or in shaping a new understanding of power but also in identifying and clarifying the power relations. Foucault thus asserted that the entrenchment of disciplinary mechanisms (for example, from the state) served to highlight the significance of the one subject to discipline. The attempt to create a regulatory system for example forced the state and society to address various social members and their expanded roles, such that the imposed discipline results in an elevation and greater recognition of the one receiving the discipline.[45]

The result is not that modernity is a dangerous development because of the greater reliance on regulations as a means for ensuring our enhanced freedom, but rather the reliance on regulations is merely one aspect of a social force that is exercising power. Power is now dispersed across a wide-ranging plane of interactions, be it the state, an international organisation, a non-governmental organisation or an individual. This is an important assertion for the international system that has to address the role and relevance of various internal as well as external factors influencing the state, and also account for local developments within the framework of a globalised system.[46] Creating international law moves to another dimension upon recognising the variety of influential factors, especially when removing the state from the centre and perceiving the state as only a part of the development.

The actual success is not the determinant factor due to the ever-changing nature and disparate sources of power that exist and inter-relate.

45 McHoul, A. and Grace, W. (1997), *A Foucault Primer: Discourse, Power and the Subject* (New York University Press, USA) at 72; Ivison, D. (1998), 'The Technical and the Political: Discourses of Race, Reasons of State', 7 *Social and Legal Studies* 561–566.

46 Scholte, J. (1999), 'Security and Community in a Globalizing World', 59–84 in Thomas, C. and Wilkin P. (eds), Globalisation, Human Security and the African Experience (L. Reinner Pub., USA).

Due to the availability of greater acquired information and the manner in which one attains information and applies new-found knowledge, there exist new modalities of power. Power results from a set of social relations that involves not only the state, but also other units such as international institutions, both public and private, as well as individual influences. The result is that power does not act solely as a disciplinary mechanism imposed by the state, but as part of the process for distributing goods and meeting the decided ends of the actors involved. Concomitant with this approach, while power is part of the overall conditioning of one's actions, it is not the sole means for regulation. Rather, power also is subject to the influences of previous and concurrent conditioning of one's actions by the variety of influences and social interactions that take place around us. As others exercise power, one's knowledge is affected that in turn will influence the individual's use of power.

Upon considering the variety of points of influence in the current international structure, one can understand how non-state entities maintain a rather powerful and influential role. For example, the power of a human right norm is not only that it represents a right per se, but also that it serves as a form of producing a reaction and creating a continuing social discourse.[47] Relying upon a right becomes the means for making a demand and asserting one's power similar to any form of assertion. Power is omnipresent due to its distribution between social networks. Social alignments mediate power such that even a so-called powerful entity like the state is still dependent upon its subordinates as grounds for maintaining and upholding power. Claims to rely on a right or some form of emerging international norm reflect assertions of power by various entities. One does not have greater control over the other but rather all are subject to complex social relationships.

The consequence of such change is that the role knowledge plays is not only passive in the sense that an individual is accumulating knowledge to create some form of cultural totality, but also knowledge plays a dynamic role in influencing the actions of individuals and their overall social relations and interactions. Such an acknowledgement of the role of knowledge gives rise to Foucault's link between knowledge and power. Power is not a uni-linear relationship since so called relations of power are interwoven with other forms of relations like social and political relations that serve to condition and influence each other. The relations of power, as developed in an information-oriented world, are multiform

47 Chapter 5 *infra* discusses this approach towards human rights in the context of the human right to freedom of religion or belief.

and are not found in a dichotomous relationship between the dominator and dominated.[48] Rather, in the words of Foucault, 'it [power] produces reality; it produces domains of objects and rituals of truth'.[49] Pursuant to this understanding, 'individuals are the vehicles of power, not its point of application...The individual, that is, is not the vis-à-vis of power; it is, I believe, one of its prime effects'.[50]

The link between power and knowledge arises from the recognition that the role of knowledge, as derived from discourse to form an ever-changing notion of our material reality, forces one to account for the changes that knowledge creates. Initially one might conclude that with the increase of the ability to acquire greater extensive knowledge, the means for controlling others also will increase. Nonetheless, concomitant with the acquisition of greater extensive knowledge is the development of more intrusive inquiry by all actors who are involved in the discourse. The acquisition of knowledge by society also will create a more insightful discourse by the parties involved in the process. While this point might be obvious, what it demonstrates is that the role of knowledge not only serves as a means for disseminating information to other actors, but also knowledge serves a material function by creating change in one's understanding and interpretation of an event that will have a material effect on one's actions.

Because power is so pervasive and has such far-reaching affects, it tends to encroach upon all areas of life and influence our modes of thinking and acquisition of knowledge. What develops from this link between knowledge and power is not power as an overarching form of exertion of control over a particular group, but the creation of an inter-linked system of influences and changes between the relating parties.

Thus, an inherent relationship exists between knowledge as a form of understanding and power as a means of exercising such knowledge. As noted. for Foucault, power is not a matter of displaying what power capacity one maintains. Power is not a zero-sum game with the most powerful being the last entity standing or yielding the greatest influence. What is significant is the manner of using such power at a particular target.[51] Foucault linked such an approach with knowledge since as we

---

48 *See* Foucault, M. (1977), *Discipline and Punish: The Birth of the Prison* (Pantheon Books, NY).

49 Foucault, M. (1977) at 194.

50 Foucault, M. (1980) at 98.

51 Pasquino, P. (1993), 'Political Theory of War and Peace: Foucault and the history of modern political theory', 22 *Economy and Society* 77–88.

acquire more knowledge at our disposal, we acquire greater capacity for control. Hence, new forms of knowledge create new forms of power.[52]

What merits consideration then is the formation of such a sense of power. Why one understands an idea to be the truth and how that came about is more important than understanding the eventual use of power. The social discourse operates within the framework of power to influence and change. Granted there might be social forces that will assert themselves at the expense of other individuals by virtue of their position. The state for example generally commands greater capacity for control. Yet power as understood by Foucault is more of a transgressive vehicle and not a form of subjection, since the subject that constitutes power is actually part of the overall mechanism.[53] It is not a dichotomy of subject-object but a matter of using power as part of the overall process that ebbs and flows with the tides of power.

Foucault's approach to power essentially hinges on the ongoing tension and inherent conflict that has been identified within international law without creating a limiting dichotomous framework. While not fully addressed, the tension of some form of objective normativity along with an imposition of subjective state interests is not the central focus nor even the reason for consideration. Rather, in a transgressive manner, one is to consider the variety of actors and influences on the same plane and account for their form of discursive developments and ongoing, and ever-changing, relationships The elements are embedded in relational structures to form a single field, such that perceiving and understanding the structure itself demands a transgressive understanding; the goal of an objective standard or subjective perception is not the defining point for a law or norm. That is, the key analysis for Foucault is not the structural interrelationship of the elements, but rather recognition that the elements are embedded in relational structures, a mutual constitution, and reciprocity, especially when considering power as emanating from a variety of different sources.

Conclusion

Upon examining the manner by which entities interact within the international system, including not only state-state relations and the formation of norms, but also interaction with other entities such as individuals and international organisations, it would seem beneficial to

52 *See* e.g. Rouse J. (1995) at 96.
53 McHoul, A. and Grace, W. (1997).

adopt a transgressive approach that would incorporate not only a variety of views, but acknowledge the role and influence of the various actors.

The purpose in engaging in this approach is not to discern the law as such but to account for the ongoing changes and developments as evidenced by the continuing discourses of the various actors. As will be discussed in the ensuing chapters, the problems noted thus far within international legal theory, principally objective normativity and concreteness, are (naturally) reflected in the formation and application of international law. The contention is that the international system would be better served and allow for a more meaningful exchange and development if it were to recognise and acknowledge the actual forms of relations between the different actors and the process being undertaken rather than seek a final form of normative determination. Referring to outmoded notions of state power and interests tends to stifle further development and can lead to atrophy of the system, swimming in the same circle of contentions that are rooted in misconceived perceptions of a state's capacity and capabilities without accounting for the surrounding altered circumstances and the fact that there are presently a number of non-state actors that also maintain a role in international legal development. The challenge has been how to incorporate these actors into the international framework whilst also preserving the international structure. The following chapters shall offer an approach towards a solution via reference to Foucault's notions regarding social relations and what can be understood as an alternative role for the state.

Chapter 3

Recognition, Transformation, and Power

Introduction

Understanding the meaning and implication of the recognition of states, particularly within the international legal system seeking some form of authoritative directive that delineates and defines the status of a state, presents an area of international law that straddles the legal-political divide. Many exceptions to the putative rules regarding the elements of statehood exist, whereby states recognise a new entity even if lacking the basic attributes of statehood.[1]

While recognition might not serve a constitutive sense in creating a state, there are ramifications emanating from a recognition decision for the status of the state and its international legal capacity along with political legitimacy and standing. These range from capacity for commercial and diplomatic discourse, membership in international financial institutions, status in foreign courts, and some form of state and diplomatic immunity. The point is that recognition maintains an important conferring status within the international realm to the extent that states seek recognition (if denied) or use recognition for their own political and policy goals.

Granted one can interpret any decision involving the state and its relation to another entity as an implementation of some form of policy or the result of a political decision. Recognition therefore is not fully understood as operating within a normative context, especially with the acknowledgment that it does not maintain a constitutive function for statehood, unlike other areas of international law where a framework of some sort exist. The decision to recognize is usually linked to a state's

1 *See* e.g. Krasner, S. (1999), *Sovereignty: Organized Hypocrisy* (Princeton University Press, N.J.) referring to, among others, India as a founding member of the League of Nations despite it still being a colony of Britain.

political policy or desire, and not associated with whether a state actually "exists" as such pursuant to the international legal criteria of statehood.[2]

Yet, the decision to recognize can bring to the fore a host of implications, particularly regarding the entity's standing and legal capacities and entitlements. A recognized entity even if not meeting all the criteria of statehood in the traditional sense, might still maintain some form of domestic legal capacity or capacity for international participation, while an existing state entity that is not recognized might be denied basic immunities accorded to states or denied the capacity to fully participate in the international system.[3] The result is a sort of odd mix of attempts to doctrinally interpret and understand recognition while also realizing the political and policy elements inherent in the decision.[4]

Incorporating some of the ideas and approaches of Foucault into the recognition doctrine could provide the basis for a better understanding of what is transpiring. Acknowledging the importance of political and policy-oriented decisions within the realm of recognition while also maintaining some form of normative framework, it is important to account for the interaction of power that is at work between the relevant parties and entities. This will be achieved by moving the understanding of recognition towards a transformative context, where a key aspect is the process leading up to the recognition decision, rather than the actual final decision to recognise as the central focus. The transformative approach opens the door for commingling political and policy decisions with a normative framework of statehood and international personality, thereby beginning to define a role for recognition.

---

2 *See* e.g. Talmon, S. (1998), *Recognition of Governments in International Law With Particular Reference to Governments in Exile* (Oxford University Press, UK) regarding the recognition of governments, where he proposes a distinction between de jure and de facto forms of recognition, the former relating to the sovereign status of a state, whereas the latter relating to a policy oriented decision to enter into relations.

3 *See* e.g. *Mingtai v. UPS* Case Number 9815088, Ninth Circuit, 5/25/99 located at http://caselaw.lp.findlaw.com/cgi-bin/getcase.pl?court=9th&navby=case&no=9815088 (a Taiwanese argued that one might infer the consent of the Republic of China to a treaty via the signature of the People's Republic of China).

4 Partially because of this mix, Krasner (1999) concludes that sovereignty is not the cementing or central principle within the international framework given the host of exceptions and alternatives that exist.

Recognition and State Perspective

Recognition presents a fascinating aspect of the international system. An understanding of what is recognition and what it actually is meant to imply differs depending on the context and purpose for which it is being used. An international lawyer for example might refer to recognition as assisting in the legal decision regarding the existence of a state, in an attempt to cloak the recognition decision with some normative content. Yet, at the same time, recognition is a political action, being that it is essentially a decision left in the hands of the state without any clear delineated guidelines. It can be based on considerations of foreign policy (does a state desire to support a newly formed regime or autonomous region?), domestic interests (might support for an autonomous entity appease constituents of a certain religious or ethnic background?), regional interests (how will the decision affect state neighbours and their geo-political interests?), and international standing (how will the recognition decision play in the UN and what effect will it have on other entities or regions?) to name but a few of the issues involved. Additionally, given that recognition usually involves a newly emerging state or government, the act of recognition is linked to the sovereign status of an entity, forcing one to consider whether recognition has any role to play in enhancing or legitimizing a new entity, at the very least within the international framework and at times within the entity's domestic system as well.

In essence, recognition is at a crossroads between a state according another entity some form of sovereign legitimacy such as to deem it a state, while also making a political statement regarding policy and desire. Unlike other international law decisions where a state might be bound to a normative framework or specific doctrine, the recognition decision essentially is left to the will of the state. Indeed, it is meant to serve as some form of indication regarding a particular entity's international status such as to encapsulate the recognizing state's desires vis-à-vis the entity undergoing recognition.

This link between the political and legal divide that stems from recognition in a sense reflects the old debate between the constitutive and declarative school of recognition. The majority of commentators have recognized the declarative approach to recognition as the prominent one given the state's capacity for integrating essentially political factors into its decision. While a state might maintain discretion, it is still making value-laden choices with far reaching effects. That is, a declarative approach cannot ignore the fact that it contributes to developments on the ground both internally for the new entity and on the international plane. While the constitutive approach ignores the ongoing process of recognition, attempts to infuse recognition with a normative capacity such as delving into the treatment of minorities as grounds for recognition in essence reflects some form of constitutive aspect of recognition concerning the status of the state.

The recognition decision does not accord statehood in the constitutive sense, given the understanding that states have largely abandoned the constitutive approach. Thus, deeming recognition as a hard-core normative decision appears unrealistic. For example, non-recognised states exist and operate as do other states in the international system despite the lack of formal recognition even when they meet all the necessary criteria for statehood.

On the other hand, recognition has been accorded importance by emerging entities and newly-formed governments, such as to demonstrate that it still maintains some form of legitimating role within the international system. The call to accord recognition in the post-colonial context or for entities exercising the right to self-determination demonstrates some form of importance to the act, especially as a legitimating factor for the new entity. Recognition in this context is understood as conferring some form of status upon the entity, whereby it becomes a fully functioning international member, with the application of all relevant obligations and protections in place.[5] Recognition is further heightened in importance when accounting for roles within international agencies and organisations, where a new entity can continue to assert its emerging international voice, especially where recognition of the entity is developing and emerging.

The question is to what extent is one dealing with a political aspect of state-state relations as opposed to a doctrine that is somehow linked to a legal element, demanding other states to recognize an entity?[6] The query is important for the international system, where the notion of membership and relevant actors presents an essential issue, being that states create and apply international law. While personality as a factor in international law

5 Hillgruber, C. (1998), 'The Admission of New States to the International Community', 9 *E. J. I. L.* 491–509.

6 Compare Note (1989), 'Out from the Precarious Orbit of Politics: Reconsidering Recognition and the Standing of Foreign Governments to Sue in U.S. Courts' 29 *Va. J Intl L* 473 (recognition as a political decision with certain legal consequence) with Hillgruber (1998), (recognition as operating within international legal framework).

also accounts for recognition, what is not clear is to what extent recognition influences or fits in to the international system.

The answer largely depends on the degree of importance attached to the recognition decision as well as the purpose or goal of a state according recognition. A state might desire to continue relations with another entity even without formalized recognition, or send out a message to the international community regarding its understanding of the entity's status. Furthermore, a state court might be forced to account for a state's recognition policy when confronted with a legal action involving the entity, such as to decide for example whether to accord the entity state immunity or the treatment to be granted to its state representatives. Oftentimes the judiciary is left at the mercy of the state's broader political goals, such as to participate in interpreting or implementing what is understood to be a political decision.[7] Coupled with the declarative approach towards recognition, which acknowledges a lesser normative position for recognition, one must consider the possible roles for recognition and the manner by which the international system can integrate recognition into its framework, adequately accounting for the importance of recognition as well as the surrounding political and policy oriented aspects that go into the decision.

Recognition and Process

It seems that recognition has adopted a more process-oriented nature, whereby one may assert that recognition is an ongoing reflective form of state policy. Recognition then is a modulation of attitudes[8] between a variety of actors in the international framework. Recognition is not solely a final act by a state's foreign ministry, but also reflects and incorporates the treatment accorded to an entity as it emerges within the international framework. Recognition then is a reflection of authoritative responses to the status of an entity, thereby including a variety of agencies and governmental bodies that influence the overlying process and underlying structure of an entity. Thus, the issue for example concerning the capacity of an entity in an international organization or body like the World Trade

7 *See* e.g. *Taiwan v. Dist Ct* Case Number No. 9770375, Ninth Circuit, 10/16/97, located at: http://caselaw.lp.findlaw.com/cgi-bin/getcase.pl?court=9th&navby=case&no=9770375 (court refers to policy of the US as grounds for discerning the manner in which to treat the Republic of China).

8 Reisman, W. M. and Suzuki, E. (1976), 'Recognition and Social Change in International Law: A Prologue for Decisionmaking', 403–470 in Reisman, W.M. and Weston, B. (eds) *Toward World Order and Human Dignity: Essays in Honor of Myres S. McDougal* (Macmillan Pub., NY).

Organisation is just as important as the domestic internal makeup of the entity and its capacity for upholding basic human rights principles. It would indicate that recognition as a doctrine does not require a definitive explication of its final effect on an entity, but rather an understanding of the process and ongoing change that is occurring both within the entity's domestic framework and externally, in the international system. Recognition will not then provide a final answer as to the entity's status or international personality, but more of a reflection regarding the perceived status of such an entity.

Recognition can be understood from an operative context. There have been attempts to identify a variety of approaches, such as internal versus external aspects, or distinguishing between *de jure* and *de facto* recognition. One proposed distinction is when recognition serves the interests of states in a facilitative or instrumental manner,[9] depending on the level of importance attached to the act of recognition and the actors involved in the process.

A facilitative role for recognition indicates a desire or choice of a state regarding its attitude towards another entity with little legal fallout. An instrumental role by contrast leans towards the normative aspects of recognition as it implies the adoption of a legal stance for both domestic and international institutions regarding the status of an entity.

The facilitative role of recognition has greater room for acknowledging the political side of recognition. Recognition is declarative of a state's understanding or intentions towards another entity's status, without necessarily conferring any type of definitive rank upon the entity. Political factors come into play that prevent any form of constitutive role for recognition, as it is not a conclusive or deciding factor, but merely assists in understanding where the state might stand regarding another entity.[10] Recognition reflects a state's choice, thereby not necessarily detracting

9 Warbrick, C. (1997), 'Recognition of States: Recent European Practice', 9 in Evans, M. (ed.) *Aspects of Statehood and Institutionalism in Contemporary Europe* (Dartmouth, UK) has proposed the facilitative/instrumental distinction. Here it will be referred to and expanded upon as an example of the process of recognition.

10 Talmon adopts this approach regarding Cyprus. Talmon, S. (1997), 'The Legal Consequence of (non) Recognition: Cyprus and the Council of Europe 57', in Evans, M. (ed.) *Aspects of Statehood and Institutionalism in Contemporary Europe* (Dartmouth, UK).

from the entity's capacity to emerge as a state; the recognition decision is indifferent or only a minor factor.

Recognition in the facilitative sense clearly is not a constituting action regarding the state's normative existence in the international system. Recognition may assist the entity in emerging, and even grant it some form of legitimacy, but it does not necessarily lead to the formation of a state per se. Other surrounding acts are required in order to entrench the new entity as a state, with the facilitative recognition only playing a supportive or indicative role in the process.

One may therefore contend that facilitative form of recognition relates to the authority of the recognized entity. A newly formed government, breakaway state, or nationalist movement desires to entrench itself and its position, attempting to cumulate as much support as possible. Being of a facilitative nature however, the recognition decision does not relate to the normative or putative conditions of statehood, such as capacity for exercising control over specific territory. Rather, facilitative recognition is linked to the (conventional) power capabilities of states and their manner by which they wield influential abilities,[11] particularly regarding the status or form of treatment due towards a group, government, or emerging state. This is because recognition is a diluted concept given the overlying political factors that come into play and the underlying issues of ideology, such as religion or ethnicity that might influence a state's decision as to how it will act towards a new entity, along with possible links to regional systems.[12] The recognition decision is connected to a political or policy decision as dictated by specific state interests, and not necessarily international norms regarding elements of a state or the internal stability of the entity.

The instrumental aspect of recognition acknowledges the role of recognition as reflecting a representative distillation of state policy. Recognition is not merely an aspect of foreign policy, but is a measured decision by a state to accord state-like status to another entity. The intention is to entrench the recognized entity as a viable international actor, according the entity sovereign like status and engaging in diplomatic relations.

Recognition in this sense maintains stronger weight because state policy has long reaching effects on domestic and international institutions.

---

11 Thomson, J. (1995), 'State Sovereignty in International Relations: Bridging the Gap Between Theory and Empirical Research', 39 *Intl. Studies Q*. 213.

12 Peterson, M. (1982), 'Political Use of Recognition: The Influence of the International System', 34 *World Politics* 324.

Recognition in the instrumental sense plays a more active role. For example accounting for recognition in the post-colonial context, particularly the call for recognition of new states in order to enhance assistance and allow for proper development,[13] reflects an understanding of recognition as encapsulating approval and enhancing standing, in a sense more than merely facilitating the emergence of the state but entrenching its position within the international system.

This is not to say that recognition shifts to a constitutive plane in determining the international legal position of an entity, but rather that an instrumental understanding of recognition points to the criteria that sway a state's decision as an actor in the international system. Thus, one also may account for external criteria that influence a state, such as human rights considerations that are taken into account by a state weighing the possibility of recognition.[14] One discerns a form of social construction of a state via recognition, where states recognize sovereignty of a state via traditional factors like territory or people along with internal aspects like human rights.[15] Thus, in attempting to address the chasm between politics and law within the context of recognition, references have been made to incorporate aspects such as upholding human dignity within the entity and the capacity to contribute to minimum world order.[16] The indication is that recognition is more than facilitative when accounting for aspects like human rights but also instrumental in moving the human rights agenda forward within the state when serving as grounds for recognition.

An additional distinction between a functional and instrumental approach is that domestically, an instrumental form of recognition will have ramifications for other branches who must engage in some form of relations with the entity. For example, the judicial branch when considering the legal status or capacity of a new entity or the legislature when considering the

---

13 *See* e.g. Crawford, J. (1979), *The Creation of States in International Law* (Clarendon Press, UK).

14 Warbrick (1997), refers to the Yugoslav Badinter Commission where strong reliance was made on the status of minority rights (internal self-determination) as grounds for according recognition. See also Murphy, S. (1999), 'Democratic Legitimacy and the Recognition of States', 48 *Intl. and Comp. L. Q.* 545–581.

15 Biersteker, T. and Weber, C. (1996), 'The Social Construction of State Sovereignty', 1 in Biersteker, T. and Weber, C. (eds.) *State Sovereignty as Social Construct* (Cambridge University Press, UK) . See also Strong, D. (1996), 'Contested Sovereignty: the social construction of colonial imperialism', 22 in Biersteker, T. and Weber, C. (eds.) *State Sovereignty as Social Construct* (Cambridge University Press, UK) referring to recognition as the reflection of the cultural features of a state.

16 Reisman and Suzuki (1976).

disbursement of aid funding. If the official policy mandates recognizing a particular entity as a legitimate state or government, the state apparatus will naturally be inclined towards a different form of treatment, according the entity the full benefits provided to other states.

A similar result will follow in the international plane. Unlike facilitative recognition where the recognition decision relates more to influence wielding within the realm of international relations, in the instrumental context recognition lays the groundwork for the application of international rules.[17] While not always maintaining all the necessary factors of statehood, the recognition decision can prove to be the sufficient push towards legitimacy and international determinacy of an entity. Thus, recognition in the post-Yugoslav Republic dissolution played an important role for the European Community ("EC"). It has been asserted that recognition was instrumental in according international status and legitimacy as a tool by which the international system relied on the EC's collective recognition decision as a guiding factor.[18]

Linking Facilitation with Instrumental

Of course, one of the key problems in attempting to delineate recognition is the crossover aspects, where the facilitative and instrumental aspects of the doctrine either merge or slough off one into the other. Given the modalities of attitudes that are at play and the ongoing shifts and changes in both domestic and foreign policy, it is difficult and even unnecessary to label a decision in any final or definitive manner. A state might be acting solely within the facilitative context to entrench a particular position, while also referring to the instrumental approach via reference to international norms or standards, or create an internal effect on the standing of an entity before a local court.

For example, in the People's Republic of China-Republic of China (Taiwan) recognition debate, part of the issue surrounds the proper application of international norms regarding statehood, as encapsulated by the Republic of China's claim to all the necessary attributes despite it still lacking entrenched international standing, like UN membership. Indeed, many arguments of the Republic of China hinge on its improved human rights record and legitimated standing via democratic institutions

---

17 Warbrick (1997).

18 Saskia, H. (1995) 'Mutual Recognition of Croatia and Serbia (+ Montenegro)' 6 *E. J. Intl. L.* 598–612; Kilibarda, K. (2003), 'Selective Recognition and the Dismantling of SFR Yugoslavia. The EC's Criteria under International Law', available at: http://www.swans.com/library/art9/kkilib03.html.

as grounds for requiring recognition by other states,[19] the supposedly key elements that are to compose a recognition decision. This is especially relevant from an international standpoint, where at least externally one may argue that the Republic of China's policies move towards a sounder world order. The facilitative aspect also comes into play however, when accounting for the People's Republic of China's threat and prevention of other states from recognizing the Republic of China, such that the latter must sidestep the recognition issue and focus on practical applications, like observer status in various international organs. Recognition in this latter sense is more an issue of reflecting international relations, where the People's Republic of China maintains an upper hand, such that the Republic of China essentially skirts the issue of recognition and forges ahead with its own foreign policy and relations. From the People's Republic of China's side, one may understand recognition as an instrumental process, being that without recognition, the Republic of China is deprived of many benefits associated with statehood. Within this essentially political conflict, each side attempts to invoke aspects of international law and sovereignty as grounds for asserting its status leading to a rather ambiguous situation depending on the assertions and perception of the involved actors.[20]

The result is that when considering the recognition issue, it is important to account for the surrounding events as perceived by the state engaging in the conduct. The perspective of the state as a central actor in this process is imperative, such that examining the role of recognition and its form of application can highlight important substantive differences on the manner by which the international system is to react. Note however that the act of recognition is linked to a host of evaluations and considerations in both the facilitative and instrumental context. Although the facilitative/instrumental categorisation assists in making a distinction at least as a means of showing how to understand the role of recognition, further questions arise. What is the significance of recognition within the international legal context? Does the status of the entity undergoing recognition really achieve an altered state, thereby acquiring the mantle of statehood? What is the status of recognition and what is its intended role if one is turning to external aspects that do not relate to the more accepted criteria of statehood such as upholding human rights or contributing to the world order? Indeed, the infusion of values like human rights or legitimacy raises to the fore subjective evaluations of states in the context of political decisions and evaluations, thereby ignoring the political and policy aspects of the

19 Huang, E. (2003), 'Taiwan's Status in a Changing World: United Nations Representation and Membership for Taiwan', 9 *Ann. Surv. Intl. and Comp. L.* 55.

20 de Lisle, J. (2000), 'The Chinese Puzzle of Taiwan's Status', 44 *Orbis* 35.

decision. One can read into a recognition decision a desire of some sort to incorporate human rights, self-determination, or human dignity, but it is dubious at best whether these aspects drive forward a recognition decision in any normative sense.[21]

Recognition seems linked to the circumstances and surrounding events, and the role accorded recognition (facilitative or instrumental) by the recognizing state. For example as interdependence increases and there is greater reliance or reference to the international process, the effect of recognition and its varying degrees will have heightened importance. An entity's capacity will not only be called into question internally, but on the international plane as well, where the capacity for full or, limited, participation can have deep ranging effects. Nevertheless, this begs the question regarding the fundamentals of statehood and the importance of these elements for recognition, as well as the manner by which one may integrate political aspects into a normative context. Where is the relationship between statehood and recognition and how is one to reconcile state attributes with that of denial or according recognition? The question also entails considering the manner by which the international system is willing to account for political factors in a system that is striving for some form of operative normative framework.

Alternative Recognition

It is especially difficult to account for the emergence of a legal norm when the players creating the norm are engaging in so-called power moves to ensure their position or foreign policy. Indeed, one may contend that in the pursuit of their own interests, states essentially shun any form of normative link. This rings especially true for the recognition decision, tied as it is not only to criteria of a state but also to the declarative intentions towards the entity being recognized. Thus, factoring in a normative position seems not only difficult but also unnecessary.

On the other hand, one also must account for the social factors that have been linked to recognition. Aspects like human rights, democracy, self-determination, and constitutional legitimacy have been noted as playing

21 But cf. Sloane, R. (2002), 'The Changing Face of Recognition in International Law: A Case Study of Tibet', 16 *Emory Intl. L. Rev.* 107 (noting the role of no-state actors exerting influence on recognition practice, including the infusion of human rights, democracy, and self determination issues).

a factor within the recognition issue.[22] In essence, it is acknowledging the importance of what can be deemed a social construct of sovereignty, whereby the interests of the population are accounted for as well. This can emanate not only from other states, their decision for example to accord recognition, but also from external bodies like international organizations who might maintain an influence on an emerging entity to uphold specific minority rights in the strive for sovereign legitimacy.[23] What can be asserted, especially when considering recognition in the instrumental sense, is that recognition plays a practical role via an influence on the social construction of the territory and people, thereby affecting the entity's claim of authority and influencing or altering the approach it might adopt in its strive for legitimacy.[24]

The indication is that recognition is becoming an aspect not only of state policy or desire, but also plays a role in the overall desired construct of a state. This construct is determined by international organizations and other actors like non-governmental organisations who maintain some form of influence on the international process and the states making the decision. Recognition maintains an effect of the degree on use of power. That is, recognition in its various shapes and guises as articulated by states and other international actors reflects attitude shifts that alter over time depending on the circumstances. An entity's capacity will rise and fall due to the modulations of recognition and its important practical and symbolic validity.[25]

The result is an ongoing pattern of changing standards for a recognized entity, such that the truth of an entity's status is subject to the regime of understanding as understood by the variety of actors involved in the process. Thus, recognition is not a final or definitive determination by a state actor, but actually subject to a particular framework by a specific state or other international actor, that shifts and changes depending on the

---

22 Epps, V. (2001), Book Review: 'The Recognition of States: Law and Practice in Debate and Evolution by Thomas D. Grant', 95 *A. J. I. L.* 252; Warbrick (1997).

23 Sloane (2002); Biersteker and Weber (1996).

24 Biersteker and Weber (1996). *See also* Strong (1996), noting that recognition is linked to the cultural features of the state and the importance attached at a specific time period to the relevant factors. Strong compares the importance of democracy, free markets, and human rights in today's construct with the imperialist period's importance that was attached to Christianity and dynastic authority.

25 Frank, T. (1990) *The Power of Legitimacy Among Nations* (Oxford University Press, UK) at 121.

perception and understanding of the actors making the case for recognition, as well as the entity and its participation in the process.

The regime of truth within the context of recognition then is a contingent notion, making for a transitory concept regarding the status of an entity, subject to constant change. Thus, recognition can be better understood in a transformative sense, not as a matter of the relationship between politics and law and the manner by which the international system can attempt to combine these two aspects, nor solely as an issue of power assertions by state or international actors. Rather the analysis is of the relation itself, what is occurring between the actors as the determinant of the relevant elements and decision that go into the recognition decision. The actual decision is not the point, but the process by which the recognition occurs, and the reactions to the decision are in essence what are important for recognition as a doctrine due to the ever changing and reactionary manner of the process.

Additionally, when considering a transformative approach as a means of understanding recognition, it is important to consider the implications of allowing for a perspective that does not focus on the decision as such but rather the process involved. Given the role of recognition as a political as well as legal tool in the international arena, how can one account for the use of state power when analyzing the matter from a transformative approach? Does power become a meaningless issue since all that matters is the process, or must power rise to the fore as the determinant factor since a demonstration of power could reflect the process that led to a recognition decision?

The latter query demonstrates that there is a different notion of power to be accounted for when placing recognition in a process-oriented transformative framework. Even with the recognition decision being considered solely within a political context and at the mercy of the states, there are still other forms of influence that hold sway over the state to the extent of influencing its decision as well as altering the position and status of the entity at question. The question then is, to what extent these external aspects play in the context of recognition, and what is their possible influence on this political process?

Recognition can serve an indicative role for the international system. Recognition is a self-regulating process in that states are acting as autonomous sovereigns thus forming some type of international norm, yet it also resists aspects of self-regulation due to the infusion of a desire to maintain specific political or policy goals important to the actors involved.

The assertion here is that the international system might do well to consider the notions of power from an alternative angle. Foucault understood power and its application as being subject to constant change and alteration. The contention is that the legally derived power of the ruling authority or of the sovereign entity as the case may be, is rather fragile. There exist a host of influences that derive from a diverse array of actors external to the state that might be using their notion of power for their benefit. In the recognition context for example, the variety of influences and considerations that go into the recognition decision reflect the broad array of factors. A state will not decide solely based on normative criteria regarding statehood when considering political interests, or solely because of foreign policy when considering domestic influences like ethnic or religious groups or regional interests and links that might force a state to comply with its neighbours and adopt a certain unified stance.

Power in the international context is not an aspect that is wielded solely by the state as the deciding force but actually reflects a host of interests and equations that go into the decision making process. Power is an ongoing development that, because it is ever changing, alters the context for examination. Of course, systems of power exist such as a sovereign state engaging in legitimate activities; but it is in a circular manner because the grounds for exerting power and making a decision derive from the sovereign capacity for autonomy. That is, the sovereign state is also constituted by the very power that it desirers to exercise. While a number of international commentators have noted this point, it is particularly the case for recognition where explanations regarding the use of state power are clothed in attempts also to note normative criteria of statehood as a basis, or more recent efforts to link the recognition decision to internal issues like self determination or treatment of minorities.

Given the multiplicity of actors that assert power or that maintain the capacity to do so, the real examination is not the eventual outcome or decision emanating from a particular state, but rather the complex interplay of relations between the various actors.[26] A transformative notion of recognition properly shifts the analysis away from attempts at doctrine and towards an understanding of what is occurring between and among the

26 Ivison, D. (1998), 'The Disciplinary Moment: Foucault, Law, and the Reinscription of Rights', in Mass, J. (ed.) *The Later Foucault* (Sage Publications, UK).

actors as the proper starting ground for analyzing recognition. Analysis of the event now turns on the ongoing process of recognition rather than some unrealistic attempt to define recognition as a conferring act of legitimacy or entrenching the state. Recognition is part of the ongoing process of development of the entity.

Perceiving power from a relational aspect allows for the factoring in of the other actors and influences on a state. The recognition decision, while ultimately relying on a state's declaration, is not occurring within a vacuum as a black or white decision, but rather develops in a manner that allows for external influences and changes, as the entity acquires surer footing or becomes a legitimate international actor.

In a sense, the current analysis of recognition acknowledges this approach. For example, a facilitative understating of recognition accords some type of status to the state by allowing for a reflection of foreign policy within the recognition equation. Recognition then merely serves to facilitate state policy, while acknowledging the host of other influences and actors in the national realm that also will make an assertion and attempt to impose their own form of policy. Recognition is an ongoing process that will not yield a final outcome but entail constant evaluation to facilitate the emergence of a new entity. Similarly concerning an instrumental understanding; recognition will not be tied solely to the state decision but also involve factoring in the surrounding circumstances that are meant to influence and at times even bind a state to recognize an entity.

Yet, there is more to consider when invoking Foucault within the realm of recognition. What has been asserted thus far merely reflects any form of process-oriented approach to international law or just describes the fact that some form of legitimating process is occurring between and among domestic and international actors. Recognition is part of this process in a certain manner, depending on the extent of status to accord the decision.

The Transformative Framework

Adopting a transformative understanding regarding the manner of relations can further assist to explicate the process. A transformative context recognises the inherent limitations of one's perceptions. Knowledge and understanding are confined by virtue of our limitations since we are subject to contingent and cultural circumstances that tend to unavoidably shape and influence our thought processes. Thus, achieving some form of understanding or knowledge regarding a particular event in essence forces one to examine the limits that shape one's perceptions, rather than seek a universal or conclusive answer. Due to the ever-changing nature of knowledge, we engage in a constant re-interpretation of events that derive from surrounding political and social effects, such that even when seeking to examine or delineate the status or existence of an entity, we acknowledge the contingent nature of the perception given latent political and social influences. A transformative approach engages the gap between transcendental capacities as opposed to finite or empirical perceptions by delineating a perception via an examination of the limits.

Recognition then represents an attitude of states and how the attitudes change and shift. As statements are made and limits imposed, new boundaries are formed. These boundaries define the position depending on a state's understanding and interpretation of the situation. Thus, the same entity might be accorded with different forms of status, without creating havoc to the underlying normative system. The normative conditions of the entity are not the sole factor, but also incorporate political and policy decisions of various states. The resulting decision reflects a certain reality for the state and its understanding (or knowledge) of the situation that will in turn serve to affect the entity and other states.

Taking it a step further upon noting the development of complex social situations both among individuals and between individuals and their government, Foucault proposed that the operation of our current condition of existence occur in a transformative context. We not only are influenced by specific political decisions or the divisions of power among states, but also serve to influence such decisions. All individuals, along with state actors, play a fundamental role in the development of knowledge and the exercise of power.[27] Power is not understood in the conventional sense as the mighty over the weak or the state as the final arbiter, but rather as an ongoing form of relationship between various social forces and actors that tend to influence and shape state decisions.

The manner in which Foucault addresses social interaction and understands power, particularly upon recognising his approach towards social relations, can provide a platform for addressing the variety of issues that arise for recognition. One of the important factors for recognition has been the effect of international interdependence on the recognition decision and how to commingle that with an understanding of recognition as an authoritative response. The answer lies in a transformative understanding

27 Rose, N. and Miller, P. (1992), 'Political Power Beyond the State: problematics of government', 43 *British J. Soc.* 173–206.

whereby the decision of recognition itself shapes the constitutive process, which is an ongoing progression. Given the current changes to the overall international structure that have resulted from economic globalisation, the movement towards some form of global governance, the breaking down of human barriers due to enhanced communication, and the capacity for acquiring a host of information via modern technology, the indication is that social relations with other individuals as well as with the state have undergone a change that merits consideration. The state, like other created or artificial entities, is super structural as its power derives from sources that are external to its framework.

A transformative notion of recognition is an ever-changing relationship between the actors involved (including individuals within the state) due to the power that political, social, or other individual influences might have upon our knowledge and approach towards a particular issue. For example, the movement towards accounting for external factors in the recognition equation other than merely the elements that compose a state are important considerations. It demonstrates that the recognition decision does not solely operate within the realm of particular criteria for statehood but also places demands on the actions and the makeup of the entity desiring recognition. Issues such as human rights or the treatment of minority groups are in a sense reflective of power tools that influence a state and the recognition decision.

Clearly, from a facilitative context it is understood that many factors will serve to influence and sway the foreign policy decision of the state. Thus, the infusion of politics into the decision is easier to comprehend because from a transformative sense the notion of legal doctrine or norms is but one aspect that a state will account for. Similarly, from the instrumental aspect, what is happening is that recognition can serve some form of normative role because the power being asserted is not solely political or state centred, but emanates from a host of actors, both domestic (like a minority group) as well as international (such as a regional or international organisation) that will serve to sway the decision of the state.

An additional aspect of this Foucauldian approach towards recognition pertains to the role of international organisations within the recognition decision. The problem as discussed *supra*, relates to the importance of having an entity represented within an international organisation or participating as an international actor without formal recognition. The understanding is however that because of greater acquired information and the manner in which information and knowledge is applied, there exist new modalities of power. Power results from a set of social relations that involves not only the state, but also other units such as international institutions, both public and private, as well as individual influences.

The result is that power does not act solely as a disciplinary mechanism imposed by the state, for example to dictate the status of another entity via recognition (an understanding that was rejected when adhering to the declarative sense of recognition) but as part of the process for distributing goods and meeting the decided ends of the actors involved.

Concomitant with this approach, it should be noted that while power is part of the overall conditioning of one's actions, it is not the sole means for regulation. Rather, power also is subject to the influences of previous and concurrent conditioning of one's actions by the variety of influences and social interactions that take place around us. As others exercise power, one's knowledge is affected that in turn will influence the individual's use of power. The role knowledge plays is not only passive in the sense that an individual is accumulating knowledge to create some form of cultural totality, but also knowledge plays a dynamic role in influencing the actions of individuals and their overall social relations and interactions.

Such an acknowledgement of the role of knowledge gives rise to Foucault's link between knowledge and power. Power is not a uni-linear relationship since so called relations of power are interwoven with other forms of relations like social and political relations that serve to condition and influence each other. The relations of power, as developed in an information-oriented world, are multiform and are not found in a dichotomous relationship between the dominator and dominated.

Power is not a conscious decision deriving from a state's exercise of sovereignty to assert a state's so-called will. The latter is too diffuse a concept and is subject to a host of influences. Nor is power defining a relationship between entities or allowing for the division of power and action, such as between the state and other actors like international organisations. Rather, power can be better understood as a transgressive notion that is external to a conscious decision given the role that all individuals maintain in creating such a reality. Power is distributed throughout complex social actions which serve to modify the actions of others, and not because a dominant agent possesses power in any structured sense.

The recognition decision then is a reflection of this relationship. It stands between the hard place of politics and the rock of international legal norms to emerge as a form of distinguishing a state's perception and knowledge that in turn modifies and influences other state actors (along with the state making the decision). Policy shifts occur as the entity might acquire more or less international benefits, with domestic institutions reacting and changing accordingly.

Additionally, power is not only influenced by social forces coming to the fore, but also of course tends to influence social forces. Power is part of an ongoing and ever-changing relationship of resistance to the assertion of power. While influencing other actors, the actor asserting power also will be subject to influences and thus changes in the understanding of power accorded to the actor. Resistance to the assertions of power are not exterior to the power process but form an important role not only in creating or shaping a new understanding of power but also in identifying and clarifying the power relations. As a result, Foucault asserted that the entrenchment of disciplinary mechanisms (for example, from the state) served to highlight the significance of the one subject to discipline.

What merits consideration then is the manner in which such a sense of power was fashioned in the transformative sense. Why an idea is understood to be the truth and how that came about is more important than understanding the eventual use of power. Granted that there might be social forces that will assert themselves at the expense of other individuals by virtue of their position. The state for example generally commands greater capacity for control. Yet power as understood by Foucault is more of a transgressive vehicle and not a form of subjection, since the subject that constitutes power is actually part of the overall mechanism. The entity achieving some form of recognition be it functional, instrumental, or even constitutive, in turn utilises recognition in a manner to influence another and alter perceptions. It is not a dichotomy of subject-object, but a matter of using power as part of the overall process that ebbs and flows with the tides of power. Understanding recognition in this manner then allows for the inculcation of political and social aspects into the decision, without necessarily removing the underlying normative or structural role for recognition within the international framework.

Conclusion

Recognition provides for an interesting study of the interplay between politics and norms within the international system. The question has been how to understand and integrate such a decision into the international framework. While international personality and the position of a state or government are important factors in the international realm, recognition as a doctrine has not been fully resolved given the host of exceptions and misapplications.

This chapter proposed to address recognition from a transformative sense, whereby the actual decision as such is not the key factor given the importance of acknowledging the variety of factors and influences that are part of the recognition process. Recognition need not be a conclusive event but is actually part of an ongoing and ever-changing process that demands an examination of the limitations to the decision as a means of defining the position of the various actors (and influencing elements) that are involved in the process.

The process of recognition and identifying the ongoing alterations allows for an ever-changing role for recognition. Perceived as part of the power exchanges that occur between the various actors involved in the process, recognition can more readily incorporate a wide variety of actors. Recognition can serve a descriptive role as an identifying factor and as a means of explicating positions of states and other actors. Such an approach allows for different modalities of power whereby one understands power as part of the ongoing discourse being conducted and not as a definitive factor or final decision that emanates solely from the state.

Chapter 4

Transgressing Problems of Customary International Law

Introduction

One can contend that the sources of public international law are the backbone of international law, serving as grounds for the creation of a viable legal system. If we are referring to public international law as 'law' in the formal sense of the word, there is a need for some form of rules associated with the international system that serve as the grounds for making a legal assertion or claim of a violation. Without proper sources, the system as such does not appear viable in any formalised sense.

The primary sources of international law are contentious however not necessarily regarding what they are, as most agree that treaties and customary international law are the principal sources,[1] but rather with the identification of their content and the determination that a particular source has achieved binding legal status.[2] Particularly for customary international

1 For discussions regarding the relationship between these sources, *see* Sands, P. (1998), 'Treaty, Custom, and the Cross-fertilization of International Law', 1 *Yale Hum. Rts. Dev. L. J.* 3; Scott, G. and Carr, C. (1996), 'Multilateral Treaties and the Formation of Customary International Law', 25 *Denv. J. Intl. L. & Pol.* 71; Schachter, O. (1989), 'Entangled Treaty and Custom', 717 in Dinstein, Y. and Tabory, M. (eds), *International Law at a Time of Perplexity* (M. Nijhoff, Netherlands); Cheng, B. (1983), 'Custom: The Future of General State Practice in a Divided World', 513 in Macdonald, R. and Johnston, D. (eds), *The Structure and Process of International Law: Essays in Legal Philosophy, Doctrine and Theory* (M. Nijhoff, Netherlands); Baxter, R. (1970), 'Treaties and Custom', I *Recueil des Cours* 25. There are of course other sources, such as the general principles of international law. *See* e.g. Bassiouni, C. (1990), 'A Functional Approach to General Principles of International Law', 11 *Mich. J. Intl. L.* 7.

2 *See* e.g. Kammerhofer, J. (2004), 'Uncertainty in the Formal Sources of International Law: Customary International Law and Some of its Problems', 15 *E. J. Intl. L.* 523; Klabbers, J. (2002), 'Comment: The Curious Condition of Custom', 8 *Intl. Legal Theory* 29; Kelly, J. (2000), 'The Twilight of Customary International

law that is subject to the whims of states and their political interests, identification and application proves difficult when considering the potential shifts and change by states.[3] Furthermore, the formation process of customary international law is rather informal and lacks the precision that is generally inherent in other rule-making processes.[4] The problem is further entrenched when accounting for the actions of entities other than states that serve to influence customary international law and create shifting alterations to emerging norms, such as international organisations[5] or other international actors.[6]

Given the changes that have occurred to the international legal system, especially when factoring in the relationship between states and other

Law', 40 *Va. J. Intl. L.* 449; Fidler, D. (1996) 'Challenging the Concept of Custom: Perspectives on the Future of Customary International Law', 39 *Germ. Ybk. Intl. L.* 198; Lim, C. and Elias, O. (1997), 'The Role of Treaties in the Contemporary International Legal Order', 66 *Nordic J. Intl. L.* 1; Maluwa, T. (1994), 'Custom, Authority and Law: Some Jurisprudential Perspectives on the Theory of Customary International Law', 6 *African J. Intl. L. and Comp. L.* 387; Akehurst, M. (1974), 'Custom as a Source of International Law', 1974–75 *Brit. Ybk. Intl. L.* 1; D'Amato, A. (1971), *The Concept of Custom in International Law* (Cornell University Press, NY).

3 Elias, O. (1995), 'The Nature of the Subjective Element in Customary International Law', 44 *Intl. Comp. L. Q.* 501; Goldsmith, J. and Posner, E. (1999), 'A Theory of Customary International Law', 66 *U. Chi. L. Rev.* 1113 (asserting the lack of any role for custom, especially within a domestic context); de Lupis, I. (1987), *The Concept of International Law* (Nordstedts Forlag, Stockholm) Cf. Vagts, D. (2004), 'International Relations Looks at Customary International Law: A Traditionalist's Defence', 15 *E. J. Intl. L.* 1031.

4 Danilenko, G. (1988), 'The Theory of Customary International Law', 31 *Germ. Ybk. Intl. L.* 9; Walden, R. (1977), 'The Subjective Element in the Formation of Customary International Law', 12 *Is. L. Rev.* 344; Walden, R. (1978), 'Customary International Law: A Jurisprudential Analysis', 13 *Is. L. Rev.* 86.

5 *See* e.g. Chigara, B. (2001), *Legitimacy Deficit in Custom: A deconstructionist critique* (Ashgate, UK) at Chapter 2 (discussing the role of actors other than states in forming custom).

6 *See* generally Hobe, S. (2002), 'The Era of Globalisation as a Challenge to International Law', 40 *Duq. L. Rev.* 655–666; Cullen, H. and Morrow, K. (2001), 'International civil society in international law: The growth of NGO participation', 1 *Non-State Actors and Intl. L.* 7–39. Cf..Anderson, K. (2000) 'The Ottawa Convention Banning Landmines, the Role of International Non-governmental Organizations and the Idea of International Civil Society', 11 *E. J. Intl. L.* 91–120 (noting the role of specific international non-governmental organisations in moving the Convention forward, but critiquing the designation of the process as a legitimate form of democratic practice).

international actors, it might do well to consider customary international law from another framework. Foucault can assist with proposing such an understanding by considering the process of customary international law's formation in a transgressive manner. Particularly upon considering the key elements of customary international law and their inherent problems, adopting a process orientation towards customary international law by examining the surrounding events leading up to its formation, specifically how and why a norm is emerging, can better assist the international system. Recognising the elements as forms of discourse between states will determine the position of the assertion concerning customary international law, such as to reflect a particular condition and the state's social knowledge regarding the status of customary international law. The proposal can not only address some of the issues surrounding customary international law's ever changing structure, but also might lead towards a more practical and applicable standard for customary international law.

What is Customary International Law?

One reason for identifying customary international law as a seminal source of international law results from its legal status in domestic law.[7] Should an international norm attain the status of customary international law, it has the potential for direct applicability within a state's domestic legal system. The reason for this is clear when considering the basic formative elements of customary international law, namely *opino juris sive necessitatis* ("*opinio juris*"), the so-called subjective element of customary international law regarding a state's claim as to what it believes obligatory, and state practice demonstrating evidence of a belief by the state that a practice is obligatory, a more objective element of customary international law.[8]

7 Note however, that deeming custom as automatically applicable in domestic jurisdictions is not entirely clear, especially when conflicting with a domestic law. Mendelson, M. (2004), 'The effect of customary international law on domestic law: An overview', 4 *Non-State Actors and Int. L.* 75–85; Boyle, A. (2004), 'International law before national courts: Some problems from a common law perspective', 4 *Non-State Actors and Int. L.* 59–64; Kundmueller, M. (2002), 'The Application of Customary International Law in U.S. Courts: Custom, Convention or Pseudo-legislation?', 28 *J. Legis.* 359.

8 *See* generally International Law Association (2000), Final Report of the Committee on Formation of Customary (General) International Law http://www.ila-hq.org/html/layout_committee.htm at 6 (hereinafter: ILA Report (2000)).

Customary international law then can be understood as eliciting constant and uniform practice that gives rise to similar expectations in the practice of other state actors.[9] If a state is actually abiding by customary international law in practice, and is doing so because of a perceived legal obligation, it seems to follow that customary international law is inherent in the legal framework of the state.[10] The obligation of customary international law, as derived from its elements, directs the state to act in a given way. From a simple legal understanding, customary international law is a force regulating the state's behaviour, such that the stretch of it into the domestic sphere should arguably not pose an issue.

Basic Problems

Despite the importance of customary international law as a source of international law, there exist a number of basic problems associated with customary international law that merit further consideration and analysis. Given the informal nature of this source of law, customary international law is bound to have formation problems, especially concerning identification and designation, such as to call the very nature of the "law" into question. The difficulty lies in delineating the emerging norm, such as to adequately capture the intentions of states and other principal actors.[11] One may divide the key problems into internal groupings relating to the identification of the principal elements and designation of customary international law, and external aspects regarding the role of other actors that assist with the entrenchment of a customary norm.

The internal aspect relates to the elements of customary international law and the controversy surrounding the interpretation and application of same. Internally, the identified elements of customary international law, namely state practice and *opinio juris* of states, have been labelled as

---

Note that the ILA deems *opinio juris* as not always a necessary element for custom, especially if all the factors of state practice exist, although proof of its absence may demonstrate the lack of a customary rule.

9 Mendelson, M. (1998), 'The Formation of Customary International Law', 272 *Recueil des Cours* 188 at 399.

10 Note that some commentators in the US challenge this approach as being contrary to basic notions of federalism and the constitutional separation of powers because the executive branch, as the principal actor in foreign affairs, is in essence creating law, thereby usurping the role of the legislative branch. Compare Bradley, C. and Goldsmith, J. (1997), 'Customary International Law as Federal Common Law: A Critique of the Modern Position', 110 *Harv. L. Rev.* 815 with Koh, H. (1998), 'Is International Law Really State Law?', 111 *Harv. L. Rev.* 1824.

11 Chigara (2001).

subjective, impossible to adequately categorise, impractical, and devoid of any concrete substance.[12] For example, how is one to gauge the emergence of a perceived obligation by the state if there are reasons external to the law regarding the actual practice of a state, such as domestic interests that serve as the driving force behind the practice? The subjective nature of customary international law makes it difficult to adequately categorise its contents. Why would a state not make a public statement regarding its belief concerning the existence of a legal obligation when no actual or binding obligation ensues or when political interests turn a state towards different practice? The impractical nature of *opinio juris* along with the variety of influences on state practice outside the legal realm suggest that the elements do not really label anything concrete.[13]

More particularly, the identified elements of customary international law appear to create an inherent loop since if a state is acting in a specific way pursuant to accepted practice, then what is the necessity for a declared obligation by the state (*opinio juris*)? The state practice element that incorporates the belief in the obligation would seem to suffice. Put another way, why would a state assert a belief in an obligation that either is already accepted or has yet to be created via state practice? Alternatively, if the state feels bound to act in such a manner due to an existing legal obligation, and declares this case, then what is the use of the state practice element? The practice does not appear to be the cause of the obligation as the state has declared its intentions regarding a specific issue. Further, how is one to discern the difference between actions or statements that reflect formation of a new rule as opposed to actions that are contrary to the existing rule? Where is the give and take between what a state declares to be a belief regarding customary international law as opposed to actual practice that might indicate a contrary intention? How far along the continuum must one go to claim a new rule as opposed to referring to the previous rule?

As a means of addressing some of the aforementioned problems, and simply to create a more practical and reality based standard, many have tended to place greater weight on state practice as the basis for customary

12 For an extensive overview, see Roberts, A. (2001), 'Traditional and Modern Approaches to Customary International Law: A Reconciliation', 95 A. J. Intl. L. 757 (delineating the different approaches to the elements of custom as traditional and modern).

13 As noted in the International Law Association's study on custom, '…it is necessary to be aware of the issue of the observational standpoint…the suggestion is that different functions may lead the persons performing them to adopt a somewhat different attitude to the sources…'. ILA Report (2000) at 5.

international law.[14] The understanding is that state practice affords a more realistic view of emerging customary international law and relies on the relevant actor in international law, the state, pursuant to the actions taken by the state. Unlike statements made by a state that might indicate *opinio juris*, state practice is an actual reflection of what states perceive as a binding obligation and thus alter their practice accordingly.

Nonetheless, state practice would seem a problematic basis for creating a customary obligation when considering surrounding factors that influence a state's action. Influences from within and without the state might force a state to act in a certain manner while not necessarily reflecting a desired practice or a belief. International relations, state interests, other international obligations, plus internal demands of various state apparatuses can significantly alter state decisions, thereby skewering their decisions and notions of legal obligation. The practice as such need not reflect the actual understanding of a state concerning the position of an international norm.

On a practical level, identifying state practice, or at least relevant state practice, is at time impossible, forcing one to sift through a variety of state actions to determine which are relevant. Even attempting to canvass the practices of a variety of states proves a difficult and awkward task, thereby raising the bar to seemingly insurmountable heights when analyzing the status of a customary norm. Identifying a uniform or general practice of states is open to a host of interpretations such as to call into question the practical aspect of turning to state practice.

Recognising the focus of the state practice element on the practice, or actions, of the state, state practice has been associated with a more descriptive, traditional, form of identification.[15] Yet, identifying relevant practice essentially ends up becoming a subjective process subject to the interpretations of the one claiming the state practice. States can easily interpret actions as relevant, while dismissing other actions as unimportant or not indicative of practice. State practice is at times hostage to the whims of the state, particularly when accounting for deviant behaviour that might call into question the notion of a changing practice for the benefit of the state and its particular interests at a given point in time.

In a sense, the state practice element should be a solid form of reference that affords a realistic view of customary international law; but

---

14 *See* e.g. ILA Report (2000).

15 *See* Roberts (2001).

at the same time, state practice is reflective of the relative applications inherent in international law, especially when contrasting the practice of powerful states with greater influence as opposed to the weaker or less influential states. The capacity for influence or alteration by a stronger state, while understandably maintaining some form of credence, tends to diminish the actions of other states. The underlying notion of sovereign equality in international law appears to take a back seat when considering the relevance of practice by different states, large or small, weak or powerful (in the conventional sense) such as to call into question the notion of customary international law as reflecting a general or uniform practice. What in essence appears to emerge is a reflection of a desire by a group of more influential states that might not encompass the practice or expectations of states in general.

The other noted element of customary international law, *opinio juris*, is essentially an attempt to identify a state's adoption of a binding legal obligation. *Opinio juris* has been associated with a declarative understanding of customary international law as it relates to what states declare in various forums, both international and domestic, thereby encapsulating the legal obligation. In an interesting twist, *opinio juris* can be understood as encompassing both the "is", since it is based on what states declare to be their intentions, as well as the "ought", since it also encompasses declarations regarding what states aspire to carry out.

The critique of *opinio juris* is that it is a reflection of aspiration rather than reality. The notion of state aspirations is the root of the problem with *opinio juris* since it is not clear whether a standard is actually emerging because of some form of statement concerning an obligation or desired standard. Will the *opinio juris* affect state practice - or maintain some form of status given contrary state practice? Maybe *opinio juris* is merely a declaration by a state[16] that reflects a desired standard (the "ought") with states not paying heed to *opinio juris* in any substantive manner.

The *opinio juris* aspect is further problematic when considering the political dimension of state declarations. This is particularly relevant for declarations of states in international forums, where one may attribute some form of obligation on the state to abide by the statement or declaration or at least imply some form of obligation. The gist of the argument centres on the utility of making a statement in a public forum, where arguably states are using the forum to clarify its position regarding a particular issue.

16 *See* e.g. Bodansky, D. (1995), 'Customary (And Not So Customary) International Environmental Law', 3 *Indiana J. Global Legal Studies*. 105–119.

Yet discerning the intention of states in such circumstances is dubious, especially when accounting for the variety of statements declared by states in international organizations like the United Nations, where the intention might derive from a reason pertaining to a state's specific interests. The fact that a state declares a desire to conduct an action or uphold a norm does not always translate into *opinio juris*, despite the support attributed to *opinio juris* by a number of commentators who refer to statements and declarations emanating from international organisations or conferences.[17] The result is that *opinio juris* is somewhat of a dubious element of customary international law for the sake of creating a standard because states make declarations and appear to desire to entrench customary standards in international forums without having the intention to do so out of any formal legal obligation.

One proposal for addressing this inherent problem has been to consider customary international law on a sliding scale.[18] That is, a host of *opinio juris* say in the annals of the UN can compensate for a lack of state practice, and vice-versa, as what is important for customary international law is to demonstrate the belief by states of the existence of a legal obligation. One can discern customary international law given a steady stream of statements and declarations by a variety of states within an international organization that would indicate the emergence of a customary norm, even with a limited amount of state practice. Thus, a lack of state practice concerning a human rights norm would not necessarily remove it from being considered customary should there exist a slew of documents and statements to the contrary emanating from international organizations or other venues that indicate a unanimous opinion regarding a norm.

While this sliding scale approach might assist from an organizational aspect, it does not adequately address the problem of political and state interests, issues that mar reliance on *opinio juris*. States might desire to appease allies or not appear as a rogue state. The actual intentions and desires, coupled with conflicting domestic practices away from the sights of an international organization or states, might point to a different understanding. While the sliding scale approach is practical in addressing the manner by which to consider the elements of custom, it also can

---

17 Reference to *opinio juris* has been particularly problematic for emerging custom in human rights and the environment, where states are prone towards supporting initiatives without necessarily according such support any binding legal status to create an actual change in practice.

18 In particular, *see* Kirgis, F. (1987), 'Custom on a Sliding Scale', 81 *Am. J. Intl. L.* 146.

remove the underlying substance of customary international law as a legal source by placing too much credence on one element without accounting for the other. This is especially so for *opinio juris* in the absence of state practice (or contrary practice in certain instances) as one must question the soundness of sliding towards the *opinio juris* if so many states are in the breach. The sliding scale approach then does not address the inherent problems associated with the individual elements of custom, but merely shifts the analysis towards greater reliance on a particular feature of custom.

External considerations relating to customary international law point towards a problem in international law as it has emerged during the previous century, that being the emergence of actors other than states playing a role in developing international law. International organizations, non-governmental organizations, and even individuals have acquired some form of "subject" status in international law rather than being merely objects in this legal realm.[19] This is especially so with the advent of transnational behaviour between states, where international organisations play a functional role. Coupled with globalisation of private entities, where the impact on the state can force a shift in public policy decisions,[20] the indication is that additional actors play an influential role in the international arena. These actors maintain an elevated position within the international realm, serving to create change and drive forward initiatives in a manner that was previously inconceivable. While the state remains the central actor in international law, most would agree that there also have emerged other significant actors who play a seminal role in the development of international law in general and customary international law in particular. This fundamental shift in the international process, whereby international organizations and actors other than states play a role in developing and moving forward custom, makes it difficult to combine with the aforementioned elements that focus principally on state actors.

International organisations and other important international bodies serve to move forward the development of customary international law and influence the practice of states.[21] Certainly, the creation of international

19 *See* e.g. Reinisch, A. and Irgel, C. (2001) 'The participation of non-governmental organizations (NGOs) in the WTO dispute settlement system', 1 *Non-State Actors and Int. L.* 127–151.

20 *See* e.g. Forsythe, D. (2000), *Human Rights in International Relations* (Cambridge University Press, UK) at Chapter 8, discussing the role of transnational corporations as influencing the application of human rights standards.

21 *See* e.g. ILA Report (2000) at 54–66.

bodies with judicial-like powers, such as the WTO dispute resolution mechanism or the Law of the Sea Tribunal, interpret existing law in a manner that alters the understanding and application of the existing norms. Such tribunals influence state practice and at times create the emergence of a new form of legal obligation that is binding on the states. Even the notion of state reporting and the capacity for individual complaint procedures in the human rights context not only cause a change in state behaviour but also lead to a re-interpretation of the obligation on the state.[22]

The external aspects of customary international law have been considered but not fully accounted for, especially when adopting a state-centred approach to international law in general. State practice for example acknowledges the existence and influence of external actors by virtue of the context of their operations. *Opinio juris* is accessible and discernible from statements and resolutions within international organisations and similar forums. Indeed, a state-centred approach will assert that international forums exist for the benefit and at the behest of the state, such as to raise the issue of their viability for reflecting the beliefs of states regarding particular norms.

Thus, the indication is that even in a state centred approach, there exist influences from actors other than states that serve to move forward customary international law in an effective manner. When coupled with the political inroads that encroach upon custom, such as misusing customary international law for the benefit of supporting a state action or overstating the significance of state practice at the expense of *opinio juris*, the role of external actors in setting forth a straight record is even more significant. External actors can force a clarification of state practice or have a state affirm its position regarding a norm because of external pressure, or assist with an understanding of the obligation and the relevancy of a practice.

At the least, the elements of customary international law should somehow incorporate the contribution and role of non-state actors since a state might acknowledge external pressure and attempt to adhere to the norms in some manner. This is not to dismiss the centrality of the state, but rather to point out the role of non-state players, especially when attempting to detect the emergence of customary international law based on events and statements that are difficult to decipher adequately.

---

22 This is particularly the case for general comments to such human rights treaties, where oftentimes a committee might extend the interpretation of a particular article beyond the original intention of the treaty drafters.

What seems to emerge from this inherent limitation of customary international law as a normative source of international law however is that reliance on customary international law does not necessarily derive from an internal drive to represent the truth of an assertion, but is the result of the utilisation of the norm by the party making the claim to custom. State practice will be identified in instances of support, as will *opinio juris* be referred to without a strong backing of state practice, where the assertion coincides with the interests of the state. There could be a host of *opinio juris* emanating from international organisations that serve as the basis for deeming a norm customary, while state practice indicates a contrary conclusion.

This need not necessarily lead one to the foregone conclusion that customary international law is a non-viable source of law. Indeed, one may turn the argument around by claiming that the growth of activities and other relevant factors that serve as indicators of a state's legal position demonstrates an emergence of some form of a customary standard or norm, such that *opinio juris* could buttress the so-called proof of a customary standard.[23] Yet, there remains the determination of meeting these standards along with the relevancy of various statements and actions and the importance to attribute to it.

Given the informal nature of the process and the necessity for examining elements that do not provide sharp or definitive features to an ever-changing standard, it is difficult to lay claim to an "objective" customary law. The notion of attaining any understanding of what a state "believes"[24] or delineating state practice in a practical manner is a non-element. An assertion regarding customary international law will inherently be linked to a subjective notion regarding a norm that serves the purposes of the party making the claim. This is especially the case when considered within a political context and a realist framework that expects actors to assert the interests of their state as a driving mechanism (thus the tendency towards a specific element of custom, usually state practice).[25]

---

23 *See* e.g. Meron, T. (1989), *Human Rights and Humanitarian Norms as Customary Law* (Oxford University Press, UK).

24 Simpson, G. (2000), 'The Situation on the International Legal Theory Front: The Power of Rules and the Rule of Power', 11 *Eur. J. Intl L.* 439.

25 ILA Report (2000); D'Amato (1971).

Reference to Foucault

Upon accounting for custom, the task seems to demand consideration of the manner in which one is to focus on the development and events surrounding the emergence of custom, especially when acknowledging the political aspects and state-interests that come into play. Thus, attention is placed on issues pertaining to not only the elements and their construct, but also the developments surrounding the emergence of the elements that would lead one to make an assertion regarding custom. This point is demonstrated by the prevalent issue of state practice and its ever-shifting form – is a new practice demonstrative of a new form of customary international law or a violation of an existing norm? The ILA Report notes, "It is not entirely possible or desirable to draw too sharp a distinction between the formation of customary law, on the one hand, and its existence after it has come into being, on the other hand."[26] States can alter direction due to the informality of customary international law as a source of law and the rather amorphous elements of which it is composed. This unstructured manner of customary international law has troubled commentators who are seeking hard and fast rules from which to develop and entrench international law qua law.

Additionally, because the elements are obtuse and somewhat general, one needs to look beyond or behind the elements and consider the manner of formation and reason for assertion. Questions like why does a particular claim reflect customary international law and how did one reach the point whereby an assertion could be made regarding customary international law are just as important as the elements of state practice and *opinio juris* since it also would serve to define and delineate custom.

Customary international law then is not an examination of the contents of the assertions to determine the existence of custom, but rather it is veering towards treating the assertions as objects and considering the process by which these assertions developed.[27] Given the variety of influences on a state's judgment, one must look at the surrounding process for the formation of a practice, or reason for making a statement equivalent to *opinio juris*. Such an understanding is generally acceptable to commentators on custom, as it reflects a realist approach concerning the underlying reasons why a state might have acted in a certain manner, an aspect that has been deemed unavoidable in making a determination regarding a customary norm.[28]

26 ILA comment at 9 and fn. 21.

27 *See* Chigara (2001) at 12–127 and Chapter 3.

28 *See* e.g. ILA Report (2000) at 13–16.

What will be asserted herein is that adopting a transgressive approach towards the creation of customary international law via Foucault and his understanding of discourse between social actors, without wholly abandoning the key elements, can better serve to entrench customary international law as a source of international law and as a reflection of current realities. The key elements will play a role by serving as reference points to assist in identifying custom, while also providing the opportunity to refer to external factors that are relevant to the overall equation.

Adhering to a transgressive approach to custom, in a manner that Foucault proposed when considering a legal framework, turns one's attention towards the surrounding events and developments that have led one to declare a norm as achieving customary status, thereby allowing for a better encapsulation of whether customary international law has emerged. A transgressive approach would shift the context from one that considers the possible outcome (e.g., is there sufficient state practice to prove a norm?) to one that accounts for the how and why a possible customary norm has emerged. Reflecting Foucault's approach to governmentality,[29] the goal is to rethink rules and aspects of state behaviour in a manner that transgresses the ongoing debate concerning the elements and relevant actors by considering how the state and other actors envision custom. Attention is focused on the manner by which these contentions derived and why a norm is deemed customary. One need not summarily dismiss the key elements of customary international law but rather consider them within a context of how they are assisting with the development of custom. One then can understand customary international law as a process where the condition is ever shifting and changing pursuant to the desires of the actors involved in the process. The goal is not to consider customary international law in a final manner by making a determination as to what customary international law "is", but to ascertain the position of an assertion such as to reflect the current condition as understood by different relevant actors.

Of course, this is a difficult proposition given the constantly shifting and changing shape that results from the open-ended nature of the key elements. While no definitive normative standard will necessarily emerge, what is important is to identify the assertions that the variety of actors are making. New forms of practice or *opinio juris* as understood by a particular state assist in moving the development of customary international law in certain directions, such as to suggest that ascertaining the overlying

---

29 *See* e.g. Hindess, B. (1997), 'Politics and Governmentality', 26 *Economy and Society* 257. *See also* discussion *infra* at Chapter 8.

shift rather than the specific assertion by a state is a sounder method for considering custom.

The point is that customary international law appears not as a final determination but an ongoing "dialogue" identified via the relevant elements. Upon examining inter-state dialogue for purposes of identifying custom, the emergence of a norm unfolds via the elements that make up the dialogue, similar to the use of language that is not merely a reflection of words or language, but also is a context for what one defines as reality.[30]

A formalised understanding of the state practice and *opinio juris* elements are not the central focus but rather, in a transgressive manner, shift attention towards the context in which the results are asserted and the indications that one may derive there from. In this manner, an analysis of customary international law can integrate a realist approach that might focus exclusively on state interests and desires without removing the principal elements. Realist notions can be incorporated into the framework, along with modern sources reflecting collective notions of states, such as UN resolutions. The reason for this is that the methodology for recognising customary international law via the principal elements are inherently linked to the ontological basis for customary international law to begin with. That is, customary international law is not only formed by the elements like state practice (as a method) because the attempts to assert or identify the elements define the very constitutive essence of customary international law as well. The analysis then need not be a structural interrelation of the elements, but rather the elements are embedded in the relational structure itself that go towards composing the structural whole via a mutual reciprocity.[31] State practice or *opinio juris* are not only elements, but are defining aspects of the structure that is composed of the elements.

Additionally, customary international law need not be linked to overly westernised interpretations and applications but rather is a more accommodating source that provides for the infusion of a number of ideas and approaches as the norm develops. Customary international law is a relative standard in a very real sense. Hence, contentious concepts like the persistent objector can conform to a transgressive approach because the assertion is part of the ongoing shifting pattern of realist dialogue between

30 Barker, P. (2000), *Michel Foucault: An Introduction* (Edinburgh University Press, UK) at 10–11.

31 Malpas, J. (2001), 'Governing Theory: Ontology, Methodology and the Critique of Metaphysics', 125–140 in Wickham, G. and Pavlich, G. (eds), *Rethinking Law, Society and Governance: Foucault's Bequest* (Hart Pub., Oxford).

states; some states recognize the emergence of a rule whilst others are not accepting of it.

The goal in examining the elements of customary international law is not to achieve a final understanding of the rule but to attempt to capture the ongoing state dialogue. Indeed, the unique aspect of customary international law is that it is an ongoing development that cannot be identified in any final manner. As noted in the 2000 ILA report on customary international law, '...the customary law process is a continuing one; it does not stop when a rule has emerged'.[32] This is an important realization, one that is essentially unavoidable for international lawyers given the possibility for states simply to assert an alteration to customary international law via a unilateral shift in practice.

What seems significant for the development of customary international law is what can be deemed the discourse formations. Upon considering the development of customary international law, the important aspect of the elements is not necessarily the internal organization of the terms or the present status of the norm as reflected by practice, but rather effects that the discourse regarding customary international law are having on the actions of states.[33] Discourse is more of a political interest or reflective of a social practice where states will assert their notions and viewpoints to create an authoritative place for supporting their assertions. Customary international law then is not a final or definitive source, but is part of the ongoing discourse that tends to influence and affect the pattern of relations and actions. Customary international law also is not a matter of attaining the truth regarding the status of a particular norm, but rather gauging the effect of the discourse on the actions and beliefs of other states concerning their obligations. Customary international law is a compound of knowledge and practices, drawn from a variety of specialised realms that brings together diverse problems, attitudes, and perspectives.[34] Something has occurred between states to create a change, with the issue being what the effects of such a change are, rather than solely considering the determination of the asserted changes.

---

32 ILA Report (2000) at 9.

33 Wickham, G. (2002) 'Foucault and Law', 248–266 in Banakar, R. and Travers, M. (eds), *An Introduction to Law and Social Theory* (Hart Pub., Oxford) at 256 noting that 'In Foucault's hands, a discourse is primarily about production.'

34 Keeley, J. (1990), 'Toward a Foucauldian analysis of international regimes', 44 *Intl. Org.* 83–105.

Foucault asserted that attempting to discern the actual meaning of discourse is a futile effort and only a transparent exercise. In the framework of customary international law, the meaning would be comparable to delineating the elements that compose customary international law. While the actual meaning is part of the process, it is not its sole substantive element nor is it the means by which to identify custom, given the noted problems associated with the elements. Rather, discourse formation can play a significant role in the developing process of customary international law by assisting to measure the role of customary international law among states. Thus, customary international law is not only a matter of ascertaining the amorphous notion of practice among the states, but also is a reflection of the social condition and historical development that serves to influence and change the actions of a state and other relevant actors as the discourse unfolds and knowledge is attained.

While the explanation thus far might come across as overly descriptive, what is occurring in the customary process is the establishment of a certain framework of understanding,[35] but not any final or identifiable notion of customary international law given the constant change and shift. Rather, what is being offered via the principal elements of customary international law is a method for deciding on what might be acceptable or reflective of the truth, an ongoing process that provides the context of operation and understanding at a given moment.

Within the context of customary international law, what is important to acknowledge then is discourse as a reflection of knowledge. That is, statements or assertions by states maintain meaning and significance due to social, political, and historical conditions that allow for the statement itself to have proper and effective meaning within the discourse. Discourse formations encompass what can be termed areas of social knowledge. Customary international law in this sense will maintain different meanings once the social and political aspects are also accounted for in its emergence. These aspects might differ due to regional or local circumstances, indicating that the importance for customary international law is a focus on the effects of the discourse and not necessarily a determination of what that discourse is. Customary international law then becomes pluralized due to the complex and varied nature of the system and because the elements of customary international law consist of multiple forms of transformations. One's understanding and use of discourse shifts depending on the perspective of the receiver and not only the actor delivering the statement, such that notions of customary international law transform ideas and actions.

35 Malpas (2001) at 137–138.

Statements made by a state concerning the belief or existence of an obligation are what the *opinio juris* factor of customary international law is coming to define. Clearly, it is difficult to discern from a statement what the state believes; but when considered within the broader context of knowledge (i.e., the surrounding conditions for discourse pursuant to an understanding of what can be said or asserted) one can begin to delineate the boundaries of customary international law.

The *opinio juris* as a statement is in essence reflecting the manner of systematisation. The statements produce effects in the context of an operation, which in turn has significant meaning and causal effect on the one making the statement. As the discourse develops and assertions are made, the position of the engaged subject making the assertion is changed and altered because of the statement.[36] The statement itself might lack clarity or distinct meaning for a legal order, but the effects of the statement on the maker and other relevant actors will create a change, thereby assisting with the identification of customary international law.

Because all assertions are relative and linked to the specific maker of the assertion, be it due to political interests or other notions linked to specific state interests, the drive forward for customary international law need not be an examination of the statement itself, but rather how that statement has enabled or constrained other actors in their utterances or assertions. The formalized elements of the social condition create a relative context for the actors involved in the customary process to consider their position and in turn make their own assertion

Similarly concerning state practice. The unavoidable relative notion places customary international law in a localized context, thereby forcing the state actor to consider in a transgressive manner what can be said or asserted based on moving customary international law forward. It provides a more realist analysis because the truth as such is unattainable in these circumstances. Customary international law is too diverse, ever changing, and amorphous to grasp all forms of state practice. Rather the relevancy lies in a localized application as understood within that particular context. The truth or understanding of the norm will be attained by the perspective and understanding of the one engaging in the analysis and their attitude towards the sources, such as for example being linked to one's functions as a judge versus a governmental legal adviser.[37]

36 Barker (2000) at 14.

37 ILA Report (2000) at 5.

What is important is that customary international law is not a result of power or misuse of position by one state over another, but is a set of relations between the actors. Due to customary international law's constantly shifting and fragmented nature, customary international law operates in a vertical manner based on one's understanding of function and body of knowledge.

In the end, what transpires is a range of discontinuity that serves to establish a position for formation of an understanding regarding customary international law based on the effects that it causes. The elements of customary international law, *opinio juris* and state practice, are the key parts of this discourse, linking it with the broader social change that will occur and will in turn cause an ongoing and shifting pattern of effect. Thus, even within a positive framework where one is seeking a source for the law, there is an unavoidable link of the discourse to specific conditions that will absorb the effects and then contribute to the ongoing transformation of the discourse with viewpoints of their own. Indeed, the emerging customary norm need not serve solely a prescriptive function since the derivation of the norm derives from a descriptive understanding based on the behaviour of states.[38]

Achieving the finalized truth is misleading and seems incorrect when accounting for the transformative effect of assertions by states. Rather than attempting to focus on the assertions being made or examining the content of an assertion, one relates to the assertions as objects in their own right, with a view towards ascertaining and understanding the process by which such assertions contribute to the development. The goal is to understand the allegations being made by the actors rather than create a supposed normative framework pursuant to subjective-oriented entities, like the state, which only will offer occasional normative solutions.[39]

Such an approach accurately encapsulates not only what seems to occur when determining customary international law pursuant to the accepted elements of state practice and *opinio juris*, but at the same time reflects the problems noted by those who refer to customary international law in

38 *See* e.g. Thomas, W. (2001), *The Ethics of Destruction : Norms and Force in International Relations* (Cornell University Press, NY) (noting as well that norms not only constrain state interests but also shape their interests).

39 Carty, A. (1991), 'Critical International Law: Recent Trends in the Theory of International Law', 2 *E. J. Intl. L.* 66–96; Stark, B. (2002), 'After/word(s): "Violations of Human Dignity" and Postmodern International Law', 27 *Yale J. Intl. L.* 315

a dismissive manner. That is, assertions regarding customary international law are in essence of importance when considering that it is the process by which such assertions are being made that demands paramount attention, and not a narrow look solely at the norm that might develop.

Following from this, one must account for external actors or public statements given the role that these factors play in influencing state choices and eventual practice as well as in furthering the discourse and creating a new playing field. Hence, the external aspects of custom, especially the inclusion of international organizations as assisting with the formation of customary international law, also contribute to the ongoing discourse both because of the influence of the state's dialogue and because of the manner by which that dialogue will in turn create an effect on the state. International organisations and other international treaty bodies maintain a particularly important role not only as a result of their emerging legitimacy in the eyes of the sovereign state or because of some directive in a treaty, but also, and more significantly, because of the role that these bodies play in assisting to develop and enhance the qualities of the international legal system.

The 'discourse' that forms a part of customary international law incorporates a broad gamut of international and domestic actors, including the individual, non-governmental organisations, the state, and international bodies. Customary international law does not solely involve a relationship between the object and the subject, such as between the state and individual or other actors, but rather reflects an ongoing discourse that is developing among and between states and other international and domestic actors. Unlike a treaty that arguably is reflective, at least initially, of a final understanding between the parties, customary international law by its nature is going to be subject to a variety of influences even before the application stage is reached. This discourse is subject to ongoing change that assists in explaining how an international actor has reached the point that a norm may be referred to as reflecting customary international law.

When factoring in the social dimension and the emergence of actors external to the state, it is only natural to include a broader discourse other than states contending that a customary norm does or does not exist. The discourse then allows for a number of actors to participate in the development of customary international law since international discourse entails a host of actors external to the state who participate and influence a state's decision. In essence, one is incorporating a broader social reality that includes external developments other than state practice as an inroad towards measuring and assessing the emergence of a customary norm.

A transformative notion of customary international law also is an ongoing and ever-changing relationship between the actors involved (including individuals within the state) due to the power that political, social, or other individual influences might have upon our knowledge and approach towards a particular issue. A customary norm results from a variety of activities within and outside the state such as domestic pressures, international sanctions or other forms of exertions, individual and group actions, changes happening in other states confronted with a similar problem, and possibly because the entire world could be aware of a particularly compelling problem. The decision for action is not merely to be explained as a result of policy decisions and external pressures from lobbying or other states' efforts; rather one may interpret the decision as being outside of the hands of the sovereign state due to an acknowledgement of a broader material reality that must account for external developments, along with actors that play an influential role either upon the state or the individuals found therein. That way, a sounder understanding of customary international law can emerge that better reflects the current international reality and provides a stronger normative footing for its application.

Conclusion

Noting the development of complex social situations both among individuals and between individuals and their government, Foucault proposed that the operation of our current condition of existence occur in a transformative context because we not only are influenced by specific political decisions or the divisions of power among states, but also serve to influence such decisions. All individuals, along with state actors, play a fundamental role in the development of knowledge and the exercise of power.

Such a transformative approach is important to consider when addressing those who have dismissed customary international law or tend to focus on the particular elements of customary international law (state practice and *opinio juris*) as the desired end result. Rather, what seems more relevant to attain an understanding of the position of customary international law as an emerging standard is to consider the surrounding circumstances that would lead an international actor to make a claim regarding a customary norm. As part of the ongoing and ever-changing process of state discourse, customary international law can be discerned via its reflection and understanding within the broader social knowledge of all actors engaged within the international system, thereby coming close to achieving an international standard.

Chapter 5

A Descriptive Moment for Freedom of Religion or Belief

Introduction

International human rights represent a major structural change to the international system. The capacities of groups and individuals to raise issues and challenge a state in the international plane on the basis of a domestic human rights violation is a significant development that would have been unthinkable 50 years ago in an international legal system centred on the state as the sole subject. Human rights provide the capacity for perceiving the international system in a broader manner, incorporating a host of new actors and enlarging the scope of the international domain beyond that of the state to include the interests of individuals and groups as an international matter.

International human rights however are beset by a number of inherent problems that either stymies its development or calls into question its application. For example, a key problem surrounds the emphasis to be placed on either civil and political rights or social and economic rights as grounds for creating a viable political structure that meets the basic human rights needs of the population. Should a state adopt Western-oriented civil and political rights as a forerunner of desired development or stress social and economic rights as the basis for creating a stable state? Relativist issues pertaining to the basis for rights and their content are also an ever-present problem, leading to issues of Western imposition of values and mores that do not necessarily reflect the cultural values of groups and states throughout the world in any universal sense (and at times even tend to destroy such cultural principles in the name of upholding a human right). These issues beg the question regarding the practical value and role of human rights as a forerunner of (desired) social change and highlight some of the subjective aspects of liberalization as a proper system of reform and improvement.

The purpose in considering human rights in this chapter is to examine modes by which human rights can maintain some form of role within society in a manner that does not necessarily eviscerate the surrounding culture, but becomes part of the ongoing social discourse. From one plane of perception, human rights can be understood as serving the interests and upholding protections for a group or individual. From a transformative understanding however, one may interpret human rights as the means by which a state subjugates the individual to pre-conceived notions regarding the desired structure of society. Certain rights might be enforced or interpreted in a narrow manner pursuant to a state's perception and existing structure. Individuality in this sense serves a coercive purpose, defining the individual and limiting the allowance for broader perceptions, both as an individual and within the social context. The result is that individual autonomy and free-thinking is actually stymied rather than enhanced.[1] Rights can serve to entrench the state and create a rather strict framework of operation at the expense of individual development.

What requires a re-consideration when accounting for human rights, at least as an initial point for addressing the variety of existing internal tensions, is reference to human rights as the manner by which the relevant parties engage in social discourse. A transformative approach to human rights rejects the perception of rights in a traditional sense as defining the relationship between the individual or the group and the state. One need not be caught in this individual-state dichotomy that does not adequately capture the surrounding processes and sources for the assertions. Rather human rights can be considered from a social discourse approach that recognizes the role of all actors in shaping the social construct. Many of the problems associated with relativism and cultural autonomy, along with social shifts due to population changes (resulting for example from a new form of minority or due to labour migration), force a state into addressing new claim forms regarding the overall desired social framework that arise as a result of human rights assertions. As such, it is important to think beyond the manner by which a right is to apply and then engage in some form of judicial balancing concerning the scope of application between the individual and the state. Rather, one needs to consider the social discourse that is allowing for specific forms of operation, along with a change in the underlying social formation.

1 *See* e.g. Mourad, R. (2003), 'After Foucault: A New Form of Right', 29 *Phil. and Social Criticism* 451 (asserting that a right can address the adverse effects of the state's disciplinary power via notions of pre-conceived civility).

Considering the Human Right to Freedom of Religion or Belief

Similar to other basic international human rights like the right to freedom of expression, one may refer to the human right to freedom of religion and belief as an entrenched international human right. It is recognised in all important and relevant human rights treaties[2] and is a constant focus of discussion and examination in a variety of international human rights bodies.[3] Academic research also recognises the importance and seminal role of the human right to freedom of religion or belief.[4]

Yet, a religion or a belief, and the freedom to manifest same, pose fundamental problems for the international human rights system similar to those noted above. For example, beliefs might manifest in a conflicting manner with other human rights. The problem is particularly acute for gender issues. One of the key problems with the Convention to Eliminate Discrimination Against Women is reservations by states with domestic laws based on religion that impedes elimination of differential treatment towards women.[5]

On a broader level, one cannot avoid the internal social structure's link to a specific religion or the incapacity to acknowledge the emergence of another belief system. One sees actions by fundamentalist states to eradicate non-state religions and remove their presence from the state, such as the call in Afghanistan for the eradication of all Buddhist symbols based on the majority religion. The nature of an entrenched religious belief within a state and the connection to group action makes it difficult to conform to

---

2 *See* e.g. Universal Declaration of Human Rights, Article 18; International Covenant on Civil and Political Rights, Article 18; European Convention on Human Rights and Fundamental Freedoms, Article 9; American Convention on Human Rights, Article 12.

3 Notably, the Commission on Human Rights has appointed a specific rapporteur on the matter of freedom of religion. *See* E/CN.4/2000/65.

4 *See* e.g. Hammer, L. (2001), *The International Human Right to Freedom of Conscience: Some Suggestions for its Development and Application* (Ashgate, UK); Evans, C. (2000), *Article 9 and the European Convention on Human Rights* (Oxford University Press, UK); Evans, M. (1997), *Religious Liberty and International Law in Europe* (Cambridge University Press, UK); Tahzib, B. (1996), *Freedom of Religion or Belief: Ensuring Effective International Protection* (Nijhoff, The Netherlands); Witte, J. and Van der Vyver, J. (eds) (1996), *Religious Human Rights in Global Perspective* (M. Nijhoff, The Netherlands).

5 *See* e.g. Brandt and Kaplan (1996), 'The Tension Between Women's Rights and Religious Rights: Reservations to CEDAW by Egypt, Bangladesh and Tunisia', XII *Journal of Law and Religion* 105.

an international human rights system that generally adopts an individual oriented approach.[6] This also stymies manifestation of other beliefs. The typical example is recognised religious military conscientious objectors, as opposed to the rejection of individual conscientious objectors.[7]

This struggle between upholding the formalised religious beliefs of the majority versus recognising the possibility for individual belief systems is apparent in the *travaux preparatoires* of the Universal Declaration on Human Rights. Some states argued for a right to freedom of religion that focused exclusively on the protection of formal religious beliefs.[8] Other states discredited the argument, calling for a more unified right incorporating 'religion, conscience, and thought'. The intention was to interpret the latter phrase as providing protection for atheists and non-religious individuals who maintain beliefs external to a doctrinal structure. Some state representatives even contended that the protection for 'beliefs' should include cultural, scientific, and political beliefs and not solely religious or philosophical tenets.[9] More tellingly, the final provision for freedom of 'thought, conscience, and religion' derived from proposals to incorporate general notions broader than religion,[10] thereby indicating the nature of an individual rather than group right. States rejected proposals

---

6 *See* e.g. Human Rights Committee's General Comment to Article 18, CCPR/C21/Rev.1/Add.4 (1993).

7 The majority of articles and books that address conscientious objection in international law approach the issue as being rooted within a formal religious belief. *See* e.g. Marcus, E. (1998), 'Conscientious Objection as an Emerging Human Right', 38 *Virginia Journal of International Law* 507; Moskos, C. and Chambers, J. (eds) (1993), *The New Conscientious Objection: From Sacred to Secular Resistance* (Oxford University Press, NY); Major, M. (1992), 'Conscientious Objection and International Law: A Human Right?'. 24 *Case Western Reserve Journal of International Law* 349. Cf. Hammer, L. (2001), at Chapter 6.

8 E/CN.4/SR.60 (1948) where UK and Peru argued for exclusive protection of freedom of religion.

9 E/CN.4/SR.60 (1948).

10 E/CN.4/85 (1948). Note as well Mexico's proposal in the GA to include manifestation of beliefs as well as religion. E/CN.4/SR.60 (1948). Acting pursuant to an earlier New Zealand proposal in the United Nations' General Assembly, the protection of religion was combined with that of conscience and thought to create a more unified right. *See* E/CN.4/85 (1948); E/CN.4/82/Add.8 and 12 (1948) Additionally, the term 'belief' was positioned alongside 'religion' to incorporate the manifestation of conceptions other than religion E/CN.4/85 (1948) Reflecting this development, the French delegate altered the French translation of 'belief' from 'croyance', which has religious overtones, to 'conviction', which reflects a more secular approach towards belief.

to limit Universal Declaration of Human Rights Article 18 to freedom of religion only, at the exclusion of other beliefs, as that would have denied protection for non-religious believers.

Upon considering the manner in which states have attempted to incorporate or adhere to the international human right to freedom of religion,[11] the problems associated with the right remain. Hence, during the drafting of the International Covenant on Civil and Political Rights, the drafters removed the specific right to change one's religion or belief.[12] Various state delegates with entrenched state religions noted the conflicts with their internal laws if the right provided for a change by further highlighting the problem of missionaries and the possibility of fraudulent changes of religion.[13] The response to these assertions, summarised by the delegate from the Netherlands, was that it is difficult for any religion to recognise apostasy, however that is the very nature of the freedom being upheld.[14] Another argument was that the ability to change related to the individual's capabilities and it was not a right granted to groups, such as missionaries.[15]

---

11 What loosely can be described as state practice.

12 GA, Third Committee, Fifteenth Session, meetings 1021–1028 (1960).

13 E/CN.4/SR.161 (1950). A memo drafted by the Secretary General before the Commission on Human Rights' ('CHR') next session highlighted this problem as troubling many states that prevent one from changing religions. E/CN.4/528 (1951) (the Secretary General also distinguished between religion and belief as two distinct concepts). Both the delegates from Egypt and Saudi Arabia objected to the right to change a belief, reasoning that it supported improper missionary work and caused greater long-term damage to society. GA Third Committee, Fifth Session, meetings 288 (1950). Saudi Arabia echoed this argument at the next GA Third Committee meeting (GA, Third Committee, Sixth Session, meeting. 367 (1951)). There was no need for a specific provision regarding change, argued the Saudi Arabian delegate, by virtue of the provision for freedom of religion that implies a right to change one's religion as well. E/CN.4/SR.319 (1952). *See also* E/CN.4/528 (1951) Memo by Secretary General who outlined Saudi Arabia and Egypt's position on this matter.

14 GA Third Committee, Fifth Session, meetings 306 (1950). *See also* GA Third Committee, Fifteenth Session, meeting 1021 (1960).

15 GA Third Committee, Fifteenth Session, A/4625, Agenda Item 34 (1960). The issue of providing for change of belief persisted until the end of the General Assembly's Fifteenth Session when initially the words 'to have a religion or belief of one's choice' was proposed and rejected as being too static, followed by the present language which upholds one 'to adopt' a religion or belief. These debates nonetheless continue, with states asserting the right to limit other beliefs if they infringe upon the state's entrenched religious system. *See* e.g. E/CN.4/RES/2000/23 (CHR Resolution regarding the right to freedom of religion). For further analysis

The result is hesitation by states when referring to the right to freedom of religion or belief given the uncertainty regarding the content and focus of the right. In a religious oriented state, a state may interpret actions such as espousing or even harbouring a different belief as rather threatening. There also is a problem within secular states. Germany for example does not recognise Scientology as a viable belief system and can treat the adherents to Scientology in a negative fashion. The Falun-Gong cult in the Peoples Republic of China also is subject to harassment and discrimination because of the potential threat that it poses to the authority of the government. In that instance, there exists a link to concerns regarding state security and control.

The problems also spill over into more formalised provinces of the international arena, particularly within judicial-like bodies such as the Council of Europe's European Court under the European Convention on Human Rights and Fundamental Freedom. When confronted with issues pertaining to the freedom of religion and belief, the Court tends to avoid addressing the inherent conflicts while deferring to the existing social structure within the state. There is little account of the influence and importance of alternative belief systems.[16] Such an approach is further entrenched by decisions that tend to delve into an analysis of the limitations to the right rather than consider the manner in which the right is to apply.[17]

There also is a dearth of analysis concerning the significance of the 'right' to freedom of religion or belief for either the individual believer or the group making the assertion. It is difficult to grasp the meaning of 'manifestation' of a religion or belief, as enunciated in human rights treaties.[18] When coming to apply the right, a narrow understanding

---

of the travaux preparatoires, see Evans, M. (1997), at Chapters 8–10; Tahzib, B. (1996); Hammer, L. (2001) at Chapter 3 (focus on the significance and implication of the treaty term 'belief').

16 Edge, P. (1996), 'Current Problems in Article 9 of The European Convention on Human Rights 1996, *Juridical Review* 42; Edge, P. (1998), 'The European Court of Human Rights and Religious Rights', 46 *International and Comparative Law Quarterly* 680.

17 14307/88 Kokkinakis v. Greece 17 EHRR 397 (1993); 16278/90 Karaduman v. Turkey 74 D&R 93 (1993) (ECHR Commission upheld university's requirement that Muslim student remove head scarf for an identification photo based on lack of manifestation as well as limitation). Scolnicov, A. (2001) Children's Right to Freedom of Religion in a Multi-Religious Society (Centre for Studies on New Religions)

18 *See* e.g. International Covenant on Civil and Political Rights Article 18.

emerges that tends to favour recognised or entrenched religions. A true application of the right, as encompassing a host of individual beliefs, is not what results from the applications.

It seems strange for a right as fundamental and important as the right to freedom of religion to be beset by inherent contradictions and misunderstandings. Such is especially the case upon considering the central role that religion or belief, or the separation between the state and religion, play in a variety of states throughout the world. The inherent tensions noted above intensify the problem concerning the potential conflicts that result from assertions of a belief.

Additionally, while the human rights system adopts a more individual based approach to the right, it is difficult to avoid the group dimension to the freedom of religion especially when considering that the right as articulated in the treaties specifically stipulates the right to worship[19] or to educate one's children pursuant to one's belief.[20] The implication from the right, as well as on a conceptual level when considering the manner in which religious systems function, is that a group dimension of some sort exists and merits protection.[21] Indeed, religion is a seminal component in the structural arrangement of public policy even in systems geared towards an individual approach to rights. There is an inherent societal significance to religion, particularly as a cultural dimension, that signifies a broader role for religious beliefs beyond the typical state-individual dichotomy, where an individual is asserting an autonomous right without interference from the state.[22] The role of religion is recognised even within states that espouse a strong separation of church and state by not ignoring the importance of some form of belief system as a social prop.[23] One sees developments in Europe whereby the various institutional structures cannot avoid the group dimension of religious bodies acting on behalf of

19 International Covenant on Civil and Political Rights Article 18(1).

20 International Covenant on Civil and Political Rights Article 18(4).

21 *See* Hammer, L. (2001), at Chapter 8 proposing a group oriented approach to the right.

22 *See* e.g. van Bijsterved, S. (2000) Religion, International Law and Policy in the Wider European Arena: New Dimensions and Developments 165 in Ahdar, R. (ed.) Law and Religion (Ashgate, UK),

23 *See* e.g. Connelly, W. (1999) *Why I am not a Secularist* (University of Minnesota Press, USA) noting the importance for secularists to establish a positive capacity for enunciating moral practice via discourse with existing alternative beliefs.

their believers to influence the state and create policy changes.[24] States therefore grant religious groups standing to present their cases on behalf of their adherents before various tribunals,[25] thereby acknowledging the importance of a group-oriented approach.

An important aspect of the right must also encompass and account for the social processes that are involved when manifesting a belief. In light of the lack of understanding or explication of what manifestation really implies or encompasses within the international human rights system, it is important to consider and account for a descriptive understanding of the process. Such an approach can serve to better assess the manner in which to manifest a belief and incorporate a group orientation, rather than solely account for individual approaches as the relevant context. The goal is not to ignore an individual understanding of human rights, but to allow for some form of social reckoning due to the potential influences that society and culture can have on religious beliefs.

This then begs the question of what is the relation between the individual believer and surrounding society. How can we explicate the social interaction that occurs for a person attempting to manifest a belief and can that manifestation be disengaged from the social context? Similarly, how can we begin to incorporate social factors without eviscerating the individual right, and vice-versa? At the very least, the significance of the group aspect merits consideration despite the individual-oriented approach of the human rights system. It is possible that a different approach towards the international human right to freedom of religion and belief that accounts for the structurally developing social factors would assist in moving the equation towards a more social context.

More particularly, offering an alternative account of the right to freedom of religion is important because the human right to freedom of religion or belief is not necessarily solely coming to protect an action per se', such as when contrasted with the right to freedom of expression or assembly. The underlying basis for making the assertion derives from broader considerations concerning one's overall approach to the manner in which one relates to other individuals and the understanding one has of their own unique role. The indication is that discerning the human right to freedom of religion entails not only the assertion of individual rights but also incorporates considerations regarding the social process. Moving away from a prescriptive context that focuses exclusively on the

24 van Bijserved (2000) at 168–171.

25 *See* e.g. 7805/77 Church of Scientology v. Sweden 16 D&R 68 (1979).

importance of the individual right to a more descriptive explication could provide a sounder understanding of 'manifestation' and a better position from which to assess the assertion.

The freedom of religion and belief, even if it can be applied as a human right in a manner similar to other human rights such as freedom of expression, not only involves seminal ideals for the individual believer, but also relates to broader issues concerning one's individual and social position. Indeed, one of the interesting developments of the past century is the emergence of religion as a key social force, contrary to the expectations of secularists who espoused the importance regarding separation of church and state. Religion seems to be playing a more central social function in a host of diverse societies, such as to call into question the notion of religion as a private individual right when considering the necessity for some form of public manifestation of religious beliefs. It is possible then that a descriptive insight into the social role of religion, as reflected in individual manifestations of a human right, can assist to provide a platform from which to consider manifestation.

Based on Foucault's understanding of the truth, we can come to a firmer grasp of the meaning and significance of religion and other forms of belief. The manner in which he addresses social interaction and understands power, particularly upon recognising his transgressive approach towards social relations, can provide a platform for addressing the variety of issues that arise for the human right to freedom of religion, and create a framework for considering the role that alternative beliefs can play in a society.[26]

Within the arena of the human right to the freedom of religion or belief, one may begin to contemplate a potential social role for an individual asserting a belief by considering the social relations that are taking place and the significance such an assertion might have on the social discourse. Consideration turns towards the impact on social relationships due to reliance upon a human right. One may remove the notion of asserting a right to freedom of religion from this bilateral context of tension between a particular belief and an accepted belief. Rather the proposed emerging broader domain is transgressive to the social structure, given the constant interaction that ensues from individual claims to rely on a particular human

26 This is not to provide an alternative normative framework or an improved legal argument, as that tends to stretch Foucault's ideas beyond their reach and intent. Rather, the purpose is to develop alternative themes that derive from his work. See Baxter, H. (1996), 'Bringing Foucault into Law and Law into Foucault', 48 *Stanford Law Review* 449 at 476.

right. The possibility is open for the development of alternative themes that can assist to explain the social function of a belief and not be entrenched in an atomist context. The unavoidable interaction between individual beliefs and society implies the necessity for turning to an alternative understanding of religion and individual beliefs, one that accounts more for the social significance of the belief within the overall social discourse.

Individual Beliefs and Foucault

In forming a belief, the individual is subject to a host of internal and external influences that derive from constant interaction with society.[27] A person is subject to many influences that will provide shape and coherence to a particular belief and even to a particular religious group. The manner in which one practices a belief similarly will shift as social influences and cultural developments encroach upon one's epistemological sources and create shifts in one's priorities. For example, the role of women in many religious belief systems has changed due to shifting social practices that has resulted in a sounder social position for women. While not fully attained, greater social acceptance has translated to changes regarding their position and role within the religious realm.

The implication of this relationship between the individual and society highlight the importance of *how* we go about acquiring knowledge. The shaping of a particular standard of belief and determining the influence of social relationships is where the significance of a belief will come to the fore. Therefore, what is important for an emerging belief is not an understanding of the relationship between the belief and morals (or some other 'universal' form of ethical standard) or solely the manner in which a belief maintains a central significance for the individual.[28] Such factors will arise by virtue of one making the assertion to exercise the right to freedom of religion or belief and the attempt to manifest the asserted belief. What merits additional analysis when considering the human right to freedom of religion is the dynamic of the relation between the individual's belief with the external world, for that is where the assertion/manifestation of the right will be felt and that can be understood as part of the driving source of

---

27 *See* generally Taylor, C. (1989), *Sources of the Self; The Making of the Modern Identity* (Cambridge University Press, UK); Hammer, L. (2001), at Chapter 4 (discussing the significance of a conscientious belief).

28 A common pre-occupation with a variety of judicial tribunals worldwide when considering the importance to attach to a new belief. *See* e.g. 16616/90 Vereniging v. Netherlands 46 D&R 200 (1986); Jacques v. Hilton 569 F. Supp. 729 (N.J.Dist.Ct. 1983).

the belief. Discerning the interplay of social factors, where manifestation of a belief becomes part of the social discourse, is important for forming a viable human right to freedom of religion, as it is the very essence of manifestation. This is not to discount the *existence* of a right to freedom of religion or to belittle the capacity for an individual belief external to the surrounding social system. However, one must account for the surrounding factors of the broader considerations that went into the individual's attempt to *manifest* the belief.

Such an understanding is implied in the international human rights system that makes a distinction between the *forum internum* and *forum externum*. The internal forum is immune from external examination by outside forces, as it comprises the internal thought processes of a person.[29] The external forum however is when the individual will attempt to manifest the belief, such that limitations linked to social considerations may enter the equation as well.[30]

Approaching an emerging belief system, or any religious system for that matter, from a social perspective might appear counterintuitive to the very nature of religion. Religion or belief is generally understood as a rather closed affair that derives from specific sources or individuals within the group who in turn assist others in understanding and implementing the practices of the belief system. Nonetheless, theologians understand the inclusion of social considerations and external factors as a necessary element for religious beliefs. Unlike prior religious thinkers who mandated that religious edicts reflect the underlying social morality,[31] present day scholars recognise the difficulty in declaring an objective moral standard that is universally applicable. The present day theologian strives for a combination of the subjective and objective elements to arrive at an acceptable moral standard[32] thereby acknowledging the derivation of a religious standard from internal as well as external influences. Religious systems therefore are accounting for the external world and the manner in which it influences the development and manifestation of a religious

29 International Covenant on Civil and Political Rights Article 18(1) and (2).

30 International Covenant on Civil and Political Rights Article 18(3).

31 An inherent tautology that derives from the history of religion as a basis for moral reasoning is the problem of how to reconcile a moral standard as reflected by a religion that does not approve or refuse individuals who are not believers yet maintain a moral lifestyle.

32 Fuchs, J. (1987), 'The Phenomenon of Conscience: Subject-Orientation and Object-Orientation', 27–47 in Zecha, G. and Weingartner, P. (eds) *Conscience: An Interdisciplinary View* (Reidel Publishing Co., Holland).

belief. As social changes or developments occur, religious systems will tend to either incorporate such changes or react in some responsive manner because of their religious beliefs. In either event, there is an inherent reaction to social developments that in turn cause a change to the religious system.

Foucault's discussion regarding epistemology indicates a similar approach that also can have merit for consideration of the significance of the human right to freedom of religion. Foucault indicated that even in more objective fields such as the natural sciences, discoveries do not occur solely because of scientific, empirical, experiments, but also as a result of changes in the political and social arena that alter our perception and understanding of certain processes; discoveries happen as different discourses become acceptable and society removes previous social or language barriers.[33] Similarly, scientific developments and their social acceptance will also have an impact upon one's understanding of how society incorporates such changes. Abortion for example had a major impact upon the role of the women and her capacity to control her body, such that one may interpret the initial attempts to criminalize abortion as a desire to control such changes in the relationships between men and women.[34]

The point is that external social changes and developments will create inherent shifts in one's understanding of events and perception of one's role, such as also to influence the development of a religion or belief. Knowledge is a social condition. An individual maintains certain information because of one's social understanding. Given that reason and knowledge are embedded in socio-cultural contexts, we can come to grasp the development of ideas by viewing them in the context of the social practices in which they figure.[35] Asserting a belief by the state, a group of individuals, or an individual believer is part of this ongoing social process that serves to form the social framework. Part of the significance of a religion or belief is not the belief itself, but the events and changes

33 Foucault, M. (1980), *Power/Knowledge: Selected Interviews and Other Writings 1972–1977* (Harvester Press, Sussex) at 115.

34 *See* e.g. Siegel, R. (1992), 'Reasoning from the Body: A Historical Perspective on Abortion Regulation and Questions of Equal Protection', 44 *Stanford Law Review* 261. Foucault addresses the significant of such changes in his historical analysis of the treatment of the criminally insane.

35 McCarthy, T. (1998), 'The Critique of Impure Reason: Foucault and the Frankfurt School', 246 in Kelly, M. (ed.) *Critique and Power: Recasting the Foucault/Habermas Debate* (MIT Press, USA).

occurring in society that prompt one to consider assertions regarding a religion or belief. It is more of a transgressive accounting of a belief that turns ones attention towards the underlying social process rather than being rooted in an almost impossible framework of individual rights that does not reflect surrounding developments nor offer a descriptive context from which to analyse an assertion.

Additionally, for Foucault, thought is not necessarily a subjective, interior, process, but is an external transgressive idea that defines an attitude of what we are ontologically.[36] This point could have rather far-reaching effects when accounting for an individual who is asserting a particular belief. We are exposed to a number of different and contrasting ideas and notions that constrain our interpretations and understanding; public ideas precede private changes. Discoursive formations arise because of the necessity to fragment ideas and new approaches in order to examine and understand the assertion. The result is that we recognise the existence of a host of competing theories and ideas, such that the focus becomes an outline on the systems of thought as objects in their own right. For example, the study of linguistics recognises that the importance of language is not merely the communicative benefits of language, but also the fact that it signifies and encapsulates the surrounding social and political background of a society or an individual. Foucault asserted that upon considering language, or other social developments, one must consider not only the social interaction that is involved, but also the social development that gives cause to reflect upon the social condition. Furthermore, language is not only a form of influence and change, but it is also subject to influence and change. Hence, one can begin to discern the value of the transgressive approach for the human right to religion. Religion certainly will maintain some form of social influence, especially when factoring in a proselytising religion. Yet, such religion or belief system is subject to constant change and influence by surrounding social factors. Permutations and different interpretations will arise not only due to internal decisions, but also because of changes in the broader social context.

Such an understanding affords an insight into the consideration of manifestation of a belief. While Foucault was fiercely descriptive, a reviewing body can better assess the social processes by understanding the framework of the assertion. The social context and development can afford more constructive insight and better reflection on the assertion of a belief. The important element thus becomes an attempt to understand the implications of a discourse and the manner by which such discourse

36 Simons, J. (1995) *Foucault and the Political* (Routledge, UK) at 89.

was formed, rather than examining the assertions being made within the discourse, because the push and pull that derives from the discourse will in turn influence another. The actual content of the belief is not the key issue, thus making it easier to address inherent contradictions between a belief and other rights or the implications of a group versus individual assertion. The subject, while an important factor, is still linked to the external ideas that are being developed and manifested as such assertions and their manner of formation are what go towards the make up of the individual. Given the difficulty in identifying the truth behind an assertion, or, regarding a religious belief, the capacity for balancing between a variety of beliefs or recognising a minority belief, what could be deemed even more important is the manner in which such assertions become mutually part of the ongoing social discourse. This is not to engage in a determination regarding the social viability of a belief, but rather to engage in a transformative understanding of beliefs as a means of understanding the claim to religious freedom.

Foucault proposed that the issue regarding the truth is one's striving to acquire knowledge, and not necessarily the struggle between what is and what is not the truth. As we accept novel uses of ideas and words given different time periods and developments, so too the social understanding of belief or the truth will be contingent.[37] Similar to the 18th- and 19th-century class struggle where the battle was not between the powerful 'haves' and the resisting 'have-nots' but was a series of ongoing clashes that formed the social body of the time,[38] a belief system can result from, or be a response to, the surrounding social regime.

One may interpret a belief or ideology not as a truism, but as resulting from the 'effects of truth [that] are produced within a discourse which in themselves are neither true nor false.'[39] The knowledge at one's disposal produces what the individual or society understands to be the truth. Truth, be it a result of experiments, an assertion of a religious belief, or the reflection of an individual's belief, is an ongoing process that need not be defined because it is a matter of continuous discourse subject to change.

A similar understanding can begin to address some of the problems relating to the assertion of an individual belief that might be contrary to an existing religious framework. Understanding a religious or individual belief

37 Foucault, M. (1989), 'Foucault Live (Interviews, 1966-84)', Lotringer, S. (ed.) *(Semiotext(e)*, NY) at 53.

38 Foucault, M. (1989) at 187–188.

39 Foucault (1980) at 118.

not as a reflection of a truth but as a matter of ongoing discourse within society provides for a more flexible approach. The entrenched religion is subject to constant influences and external exertions that would suggest the occurrence of ongoing change. The truth is not what is attained but rather what is reflected in the continuing discourse, such that the entrenched religion or newly asserted belief are not truth in themselves but rather an exercise of what the individual understands to be the truth. Hence, the inherent tension between an entrenched belief and a potentially conflicting individual belief is not a threat per se to the majority religion, but rather is a form of maintaining ongoing discourse between social elements.

Foucault's descriptive understanding provides the contextual element that can serve to define many of the problems relating to freedom of religion and better assessment of the manifestation of a belief. The development of a belief could be the result of a host of influences based on our particular regime of understanding; a belief need not relate to the truth of one's existence or to some lofty ethical standard. Rather, asserting a belief that differs from the accepted religious structure of society is indicating another way in which we can understand the truth. Similarly, a state must also realise that its conception of religious reality is subject to change. It too is not a reflection of the truth but a development that is subject to the social forces and social changes given the ongoing push and pull between individuals within the state who assert their power in different forms. While the exteriority is limited for an individual belief since it emanates from the individual's subjective understanding of the changes and discourses surrounding the individual, social factors also tend to influence and shape one's internal belief structure.[40] Relying on a belief need not entail an individual's strive for the search for a universal truth, but rather can be understood as an ongoing search for a new understanding of one's position in the world and a sharper focus on the freedom that defines an individual's distinguished role in life.[41]

The key factor then is to acknowledge our derivation of knowledge and understand our social interactions, with a view towards shaping a new

40 Walzer, M. (2001), *Universalism and Jewish Values* transcript of 15/5/01 speech at http://www.cceia.org/viewMedia.php/prmID/114 makes a similar point in discussing universality within Judaism.

41 Bernauer, J. and Mahon, M. (1994), 'The Ethics of Michel Foucault', 153 in Gutting, G. (ed.) *The Cambridge Companion to Foucault* (Cambridge University Press, USA).

understanding of ourselves.[42] All entities exercising power, or espousing the right to a particular belief system, are part of a broader framework of social relations. This assists to identify the underlying goal when considering a belief. As the external world shifts and different alternatives become available, one's approach to the truth of a particular belief will also be subject to change. Beliefs then become contingent ideas, given different levels of knowledge and understanding in societies.

Contrasting Two Cases

An example of the implications of this proposed approach is two decisions from the European Court on Human Rights. In *Cha'are Shalom Ve Tsedek v. France*,[43] the applicant claimed that the French Government had violated Article 9 (freedom of religion or belief) of the European Convention on Human Rights and Fundamental Freedoms ('ECHR'). France had refused to register the claimant's organisation as legally capable of carrying out the ritual slaughtering of animals in accordance with the claimant's strict interpretation of the Jewish law. This minority faction was acting pursuant to their unique application of Jewish law that differed from the majority of the rest of the Jewish community in France.[44] The Court decided in favour of France by holding that the minority faction within the Jewish community need not engage in their more stringent method of slaughter because they could obtain such meat from sources outside the country. The Court therefore held that there was no interference with the manifestation of a religion or belief.[45] Furthermore, the Court noted that it was imperative

---

42 Rouse J. (1994), 'Power/Knowledge', 111 in Gutting, G. (ed.) *The Cambridge Companion to Foucault* (Cambridge University Press, USA) noting that understanding Foucault as striving for an ongoing process of attaining truth can begin to address critics such as Taylor and Rorty, whose analyses were tied to the epistemic or political sovereign such that they could not avoid the conclusion that Foucault was caught in a never-ending cycle of power.

43 27417/95 *Cha'are Shalom Ve Tsedek v. France* Decision of 27/6/00.

44 The issue entailed state regulation of the Jewish 'shechita' process, whereby animals are slaughtered pursuant to the demands of the religion. The Government had regulated this ritualistic slaughtering process in order to minimise any undue pain to the animals, with only one religious authority that represented the majority of the Jewish community being granted permission to carry out slaughter in accordance with the Jewish law. The minority faction claimed that its method more fully adhered to the Jewish law particularly as it required rigorous inspections of the internal organs of the slaughtered animal.

45 27417/95 *Cha'are Shalom Ve Tsedek v. France* Decision of 27/6/00 at paragraph 83.

for France to impose public order, especially when addressing the matter of promoting religious harmony and tolerance.[46]

While this case personifies the manner in which the ECHR Court has tended to address religious issues, it is also interesting in that the Court seemed to overlook the importance of the social discourse that was occurring between the majority and minority factions within the Jewish community. The factions differed as to the proper scope of various Jewish legal edicts. In essence, the factions were raising the issue of what is the 'true' opinion for ritual slaughter. Upon considering manifestation of a belief, it is important to recognise that the assertions are subject to ongoing dialogue and constant change. This point was alluded to in the dissent when stating that the seminal issue actually was that of upholding pluralism within society by providing for the manifestation of a particular belief, rather than dismissing the minority faction's assertion due to the possibility of acquiring meat from outside the country.[47] The minority faction in *Cha'are Shalom* believed that the Jewish law required a more stringent approach to ritual slaughter, such that it attempted to manifest that belief by asserting a right to conduct slaughter pursuant to that approach.

Even more so, however, the Court should have taken into account the surrounding factors that led up to the manifestation. A group of individuals deemed a particular form of ritual slaughter to be a method that did not conform to their beliefs. It was not an issue of accounting for the potential to achieve a compromise within the Jewish community or even the right to assert fiscal control over the received taxes from the slaughtering process,[48] but rather a matter of understanding the context in which the claimant raised the assertions. Particularly when considering the importance of a religion or belief, the desire to manifest it because of the accumulation of knowledge will have a profound affect on the actions of others. The minority faction in *Cha'are Shalom* then was acting to manifest its belief that in turn will create an internal change within the overall Jewish community concerning the manner of ritual slaughter. Due to changes within the social discourse of the Jewish community, there arose a necessity by the minority faction to adopt a more stringent stance in interpreting the dictates of the Jewish law. In essence, this minority faction is part of the ongoing discourse regarding

---

46 *Id.* at paragraph 84.

47 One wonders whether the Court would uphold a complete ban on such ritual slaughter using the same reasoning (i.e., that acts of slaughter are not deemed a manifestation of a religious belief).

48 These are points that the majority of the Court alluded to in its discussion, based on the contentions of the State.

the accorded interpretation of the Jewish law and to the meaning of what it is to manifest a belief. Therefore, the assertion by this minority faction within the Jewish community is essentially within the social context of what it means to manifest a belief, such that a supposedly pluralistic state would inherently provide for the manifestation of the belief rather than dismiss the right.

By contrast, in *Valsamis v. Greece*,[49] a school suspended a child of a Jehovah Witness for not attending a public celebration of the outbreak of World War Two outside of school hours. The commemoration proved to be an obstacle for the child due to the presence and participation of Church and military authorities at the parade.[50] In essence, the claim was one of non-manifestation, in that attending the parade tended to conflict with her inherent belief system. Nonetheless, the Court held that because the parade was a mere commemoration, the military presence was minor, and the parents can easily enlighten the child as to their beliefs, there was no violation of Article 9 of the Treaty.[51]

As in the *Cha'are Shalom Ve Tsedek v. France* case, the Court ignored the importance of social discourse that resulted from the Valsamis' claims. The assertion was based on the implications that would derive within the social discourse concerning the position of Jehovah Witnesses and their relationship with military authorities. Similar to the point noted by the dissent, the issue was a matter of not participating in an event that was contrary to their beliefs, such that according the parade a commemorative status ignores the claimant's assertion.

For the Valsamis' or for the minority Jewish faction in *Cha'are Shalom*, the asserted truth was a result of their subjective understanding, such that in light of the absence of any grounds for imposing a limitation pursuant to ECHR Article 9(2), there was no basis for preventing the manifestation of the belief. The manifestation was an inherent and seminal part of the ongoing social discourse that gives rise to new meanings and interpretations of the belief system. Foucault's proposal of a transgressive understanding to describe instances of social relations opens the door for a reviewing body to consider a belief without weighing the merits or significance of the belief. Rather, one can begin to understand the manifestation via

49 74/1995/580/666 *Valsamis v. Greece* 1996-VI Rep. Judg. & Dec. 2312.

50 *Id.* at paragraph 9. Note that the parents also referred to Optional Protocol No 1, Article 2 (regarding the right to education) as well as Article 9 of the European Convention, at paragraph 21.

51 *Id.* at paragraph 37, referring to paragraph 31.

consideration of the function of the assertion and the social significance of these assertions for the individual and particular group. Attention is turned towards the social role of beliefs, such as to transgress the individual context, by considering how these new assertions arose and what their social position is. How will assertions affect future understanding of manifestation and what can be understood from these manifestations concerning social discourse? What is the approach to the asserted belief and how does that encapsulate a current understanding of the contingent truth, which will certainly alter as new forms of manifestations arise?

The question then is, even with an understanding of religion or belief as a form of ongoing social discourse, particularly when considering the manifestation of a belief in an external context, what is the meaning and significance of the human right? That is, why even bother to engage in rights discourse if we are treating the assertion of a belief as a reflection of an ongoing and ever shifting understanding of the truth? It would seem sufficient to merely deem the assertion of a belief as a matter of discourse and let the cards fall as they may. If a believer happens to reside in an oppressive society then the form of discourse between the governmental authorities and the individual will radically differ than an individual residing in a more open or so-called tolerant society. Alternatively, one can let the matter lie with the responsibility of the courts, as in the aforementioned cases, to determine the scope of a pluralist society, especially when considering the state's assertions as being part of the ongoing and more general discourse pertaining to the structure of society. France might not desire to recognise a new minority faction given the possible implications for other minority groups who might begin to assert their particular views,[52] while Greece might deem it inherently important that its citizens participate in a parade marking a national holiday. The development of the truth will simply differ as it is subject to different influences, such that the designation of an assertion of religion or belief as a right seems irrelevant.[53] Of course, the minority faction or religious group might take part in the social dialogue and even assist with forging the religious landscape of the state, but it would seem that the ultimate arbiter should be the state or another external apparatus.

52 *See also* Parekh, B. (2000), *Rethinking Multiculturalism: Cultural Diversity and Political Theory* (Macmillan Press, London) at 6–7 noting France's problems with acknowledging the possibility of a multicultural society, to the extent that it reserved on Article 27 of the International Covenant on Civil and Political Rights.

53 Arguably one can claim that the context is simply one of free expression, pursuant to an understanding of expression as striving for truth.

Furthermore, even with a different approach to religion and belief, there remain continuing tensions and conflict between asserting an individual belief and the perceived potential dangers for the broader social structure or an entrenched majority religion. We are left with the issue of how is this approach different at least regarding our understanding of the relationship between the various social players? How can this difference assist to alleviate some of the inherent tension that results from conflicting beliefs? The answer will lie in the recognition that factors external to the state are fundamental in creating social change, particularly when considering Foucault's approach to power and knowledge.

Within the context of human rights, the dichotomous relationship between the sovereign state and the individual according to Foucault is misplaced. The focus is not on the sacrifice or deference to the sovereign entity or what is the scope of power available to the sovereign state. These are issues that pertain to the eventual domination or use of power that result from an entity having the capacity for power, or, to use the language of Foucault, as a result of an entity asserting what it understands to be the truth concerning its role and status as a means of exercising its power. The sovereign entity is part of the overall power framework not because it is the final 'power user' but because of the manner in which it uses power and how power is used against it. That is, the state, like any other user of power is not above the power framework but actually part of that framework. The result is that a transgressive approach moves a reviewing body to consider the broader interplay among the various actors and the implementation of their understanding of knowledge within society.

For Foucault, the state is a creation of our discourses and is not representative of a unified whole. The state can be understood in a historical sense as being the result of an attempt to de-personalise our forms of relationships.[54] Because power is coextensive with all forms of relationships, the state is merely one aspect of such power relationships given the possibility for influence as well as to be influenced by the actions of others. The state is merely another spoke in the wheel and not necessarily the wheel itself.

---

54 Constable, M. (1991) 'Foucault and Walzer: Sovereignty, Strategy and the State', 24 *Polity* 268

Implications for the Right to Freedom of Religion or Belief

Pursuant to an understanding of power and knowledge as creating an ongoing form of interaction and influence, asserting the right to freedom of religion or belief will also be of more tactical use since the human right is a form of asserting oneself and using the available power tools.[55] One's subjective understanding of discourse regarding the truth or a belief can become a powerful tool in shaping and influencing society and producing a particular effect.[56] This transformative process places the focus not on bilateral oppositions, but rather on the notion of perpetual differences. One should not only discern what 'is', but also how the 'is' becomes a transformable unit.[57] Social interactions, in particular religious or individual beliefs, derive from discourses that influence, but also have been influenced, by surrounding social factors. The significance of this is that we do not only alter our modes of operations because of a particular belief but, because of the transformative process, we also modify the rules of formation.

The implication of Foucault's structuring social interaction based on power is the relegation of individual liberty and autonomy to being a minor factor. Individual liberty could be construed as the flipside of state sovereignty whereby just as sovereignty is a term that does not describe the true relationship and power structuring between the state and the individual, so too concerning individual liberty. The individual asserting a claim to liberty via the exercise of a right is simply utilising the same power relationship that existed between the individual and the state. The description does not reflect the underlying reality or the inherent link between power and knowledge.

Yet, what is important for Foucault, and for our understanding of the significance of the freedom of religion or belief as a human right, is that individuals critically evaluate and modify systems. Autonomy is a form of aesthetic self-invention rather than striving for a universal understanding of the truth.[58] Liberty is an internal notion focused on the self, whereas the social interaction that derives from asserting a belief or exercising a right is part of the strategic interaction that brings to the fore the use of power.

55 Ivison (1998).

56 Foucault (1977) at 123.

57 McHoul and Grace (1997).

58 McCarthy (1998) at 268–269 noting however the distinction between some of Foucault's earlier works that tended to treat the individual as a nodal point that shied away from subjectification in favour of seeking overall networks of power.

One can approach religion or belief in a manner similar to the construct proposed by Foucault regarding power and knowledge, especially when considering the conflict that arises between states and emerging religious or individual beliefs. The development of religion or belief is a result of alterations in our understanding. As we strive for a specific social understanding that derives from a religion or belief, we see an emergence in which the individual is making use of one's knowledge within the context of exercising power. Because the achievement of truth is part of the eventual goal for a religious or individual believer, the assertion of a belief is in a sense a personification of what that individual understands to be the truth. In a broader sense, the assertion is a part of the social discourse that goes towards contributing to the overall knowledge.[59] This knowledge is asserted against society not only as a power tool so to speak, but also as a means of effecting change in society's understanding of the truth. In turn of course, society, the majority, or other forces will respond with their understanding of the truth as well as with the view towards asserting its knowledge that might emanate from a more accepted religious belief and with the attempt to assert its power as well over other individuals. That is part of the interlinked system of influences between power and knowledge.

Upon considering the manner in which one is to uphold the rights of varied belief interests, the issue is not a matter of balancing rights between say an accepted religion and a minority group or a discriminatory practice and freedom of religion, but rather one can comprehend an interplay of social reactions among various individuals. Because we all maintain some form of power whose purpose is not to subject others or dominate others with our views[60] but to create some form of social change, individual beliefs maintain a significant social effect. A reviewing body considering manifestation of a belief need not focus solely on the individual assertion of a right, but on the manner in which the assertion plays a role in the social process. For example, the European Court in *Cha'are Shalom* and *Valsamis* would have done better to acknowledge the role that these minority bodies play within the social discourse. Manifestations are assertions of power that pertain to conditioning the actions of others and contribute to the social dialogue; they need not be understood as individual assertions that require state oversight. Denying the assertions for reasons like acquisition of meat

---

59 *See* Strenski, I. (1998), 'Religion, Power, and Final Foucault', 66 *J. American Academy of Rel.* 345 noting that the consideration of Foucault and religion need not involve assertions of religion as reflecting a dominant power structure, but in a more positive light, as part of the ongoing discourse.

60 Although the possibility of domination is ever present.

from outside the state or the capacity for parents to explain their beliefs to a child despite action to the contrary does not address the asserted right but rather avoids the issue. It is important to acknowledge the social function of these beliefs both in forming additional avenues of understanding and in recognising the necessity for social development. Laws or rights are inadequate in this sense because they are not a final address to assert against the state but rather are a tool used in the broader social struggle to assert oneself in shaping and structuring the practices of the political order.[61] Hence, the role of the minority belief is significant, such as to call into play issues like why did such an assertion arise and to consider the broader social interplay of the minority belief.[62]

In demonstrating an alternative form of approach towards social interactions in general and in the relationship between the individual and the state, an assertion of a religious belief takes on a different level of understanding. One need not assess the manifestation of a belief that conflicts with an entrenched religion as a social struggle whereby the more powerful force dominates or the religion more closely linked to the state prevails. Adopting a transgressive approach allows for an understanding of such social interaction as an attempt at amelioration within society. The belief that is being asserted is to be considered within the broader social framework, from outside the social sphere and from within the belief itself. The actual merits of the belief are not the focus but the formulation of the belief is what matters. In essence, beliefs are contingent and represent an ongoing discourse between social elements. The battle or struggle is not between the state and individual or between social forces, but entails a broader vista than is being played out as various individuals assert their rights.

A minority faction within a religion or belief system then will attempt to manifest a belief, whether it is correct or not. What matters however is the recognition of the importance of such assertions for the overall social discourse. This can also assist societies in transition, such as in many European countries with a burgeoning Muslim population. One may understand new assertions of beliefs, like wearing a headscarf to school or refusing to participate in a national commemoration, in a transgressive manner.

---

61 Ivison (1998).

62 Note that this is not meant to serve as an acknowledgment of the margin of appreciation as deference to the state. It is the opposite – the social construct actually derives from a host of sources and influences that are external to the state and its capacity.

A recent example in the European context that in a sense personifies these issues is the European Court of Human Rights case *Sahin v. Turkey*.[63] Sahin was denied the right to wear a headscarf in accordance with her religious beliefs since the university deemed it a threat to the public order (especially as creating tension with non-believers) and contrary to the constitutional principle of secularism. While the Court recognized the headscarf as a proper manifestation of a religious edict,[64] it deferred to the state's domestic law as acting to uphold a legitimate and necessary aim within democratic society.[65] Specifically, the Court deemed the state as the key neutral actor sufficient to determine the means for upholding public order and preserving the basic principles of secularism and equality vital to democratic survival.[66] Mere deference to a state's underlying principle of secularism however does not translate into grounds for limiting manifestation of a belief in a university. Indeed, one can contend that it reflects the very opposite of a secularist society – especially within the confines of a university where ideas and notions are to be discussed and refined. The reliance on the right is reflecting ideas and ideals of a particular group that assists in composing social discourse as well as overall knowledge.

In applying the right to manifest a belief, the general tendency to focus on the belief and determine whether it conforms to the intentions of the treaty drafters, or is a so-called viable belief in the social system, is misplaced. Rather it might do well to consider why a particular belief came about, what is occurring within the social framework such as to witness the emergence of a belief, and how did the belief emerge. While these questions are somewhat awkward, they tend to focus on the relevant questions concerning the right to freedom of religion. As a result of the diffusion of power across the broad spectrum of society, the entitlement of all social forces to assert a belief is part of this larger dynamic.

To turn to the state construct or to rely on a margin of appreciation doctrine as grounds for limiting a belief or defining the right to freedom of religion is overly narrow. The problems noted at the outset rise to the fore. Judicial tribunals must look beyond the temptation to engage in some

63 44774/98 *Leyla Sahin v. Turkey* decided 10/11/05 available at: http://cmiskp.echr.coe.int/tkp197/viewhbkm.asp?action=open&table=1132746FF1FE2A468ACCBCD1763D4D8149&key=17671&sessionId=5856548&skin=hudoc-en&attachment=true (hereinafter: Sahin).

64 Sahin at para. 78.

65 Sahin at para. 110.

66 Sahin at para. 111.

form of social balancing by considering the broader social interplay that is at work. For example, a margin of appreciation doctrine could account for the social roles of all individuals who are involved in social discourse, including the individual believer, and not merely rely on state assertions regarding the desired social construct.[67] The role of power derives from all individuals not just the state, such that all actors maintain a level of importance when considering the manifestation of beliefs.

Conclusion

A key factor in proposing an alternative understanding of the human right to freedom of religion and belief is that the context of the right is not to be solely understood as clashes between two opposing social forces, such as the state versus the individual, two opposing belief systems, or between a religious belief and another human right. Each component should be understood as maintaining a capacity for assertion. Rather, it is an issue of asserting power and recognising that all social forces including the state are part of this process, not above it.

Given the enhanced role of individuals and other non-governmental and international entities resulting from the international human rights system, the capacity for asserting one's power takes on a different dimension. Human rights are not perceived as a struggle of wills between the state and individual, whereby power is conceived in a bilateral sense between the two. Rather, given the broad-form approach to power and the inherent link between power and knowledge, human rights are a means to engage the social discourse in providing a shape and context to society. The apparent influential capacity that all actors play in defining and shaping society indicates the necessity for a different approach to the right to freedom of religion as well. A new belief or a minority belief has an important role to play within society, as does a contrary view or an externally affected group. The suggested approach includes within the equation social considerations apart from state interests. Adhering to a descriptive framework, it is important to recognise these social developments in a transformative sense as part of the overall social change, and not as outside elements that are to be avoided or deemed insignificant to an individual-oriented human rights system.

---

67 Prebensen, S. (1998), 'The Margin of Appreciation and Articles 9, 10 and 11 of the Convention '19 *Human Rights Law Journal* 13.

Chapter 6

Human Security from a Transformative Context

Introduction

International human rights served as an example that shifted attention towards individual rights, placing the individual as a subject of the international legal system. International human rights however is not the only system that created change and development within the international system. There have been a number of proposed concepts that have attempted to reflect and encompass the changes occurring to the manner of international relations and emerging international standards that have encompassed a number of actors outside the state. Further changes have occurred as well however when considering for example environmental matters, development issues, or poverty as being within the purview of the international system. Such matters place many domestic concerns and the internal political and social construct onto the international plane, while not always considering the process by which this is to occur nor the effect that such shifts can have on an international system rooted in the importance of state sovereignty.

Many times, normative gaps exist between the desired ends of a specific program or initiative and the means by which to achieve results. The international system tends to establish high goals to eradicate social ills such as poverty or disease without properly accounting for the seminal shifts that are demanded in the approach towards addressing these issues and creating an alternative construct that would better serve the desired ends.

In response to the changes in focus within the international system, as well as recognising the broader form issues that are of central concern, proposals have been made to shift away from the state as a central actor and properly account for the various groups and individuals in a more direct manner. One aspect in particular has been to consider the notion of a security in a more human-oriented manner that would broaden an understanding of what security implies and allow for a wider variety of programs and initiatives that meet the immediate needs of populations in distress. This approach has been referred to as human security.

Human security can be an important and central concept for addressing a range of seminal yet troubling topics, as well as dealing with various lacunae, within the international system. One key approach that would allow for the operation of a human security paradigm within international law is as a means of providing an underlying context for bridging the gap between intersecting normative systems. Many emergent concepts that propose or institute new forms of standards or direction for states, or incorporate external actors, merit some form of contextual backdrop. Environment and ecological matters, civil conflicts and gaps in humanitarian norms (especially when integrating human rights or non-state actors, or considering internal conflicts), development issues and their relationship with human rights, as well as approaches to globalization can be areas within international law that would benefit from a human security approach. The reason is that human security in essence allows for a perspective that adopts interests and concerns beyond the context of state–state relations, where security might imply military or economic might, and expands upon the meaning and implication of security within a different context.

Reference to human security that points towards a broader, more encompassing, notion of security is not only because of a need for a reference point, but also due to the realization that a variety of international issues and concerns are heavily interconnected. For example, when considering globalization and the call for a market oriented economy as a means of improving the economic position of a state and promoting stability, one also must consider distribution issues and the manner in which the social economy operates. As noted by the United Nations Commission on Human Security, the question is not whether to utilise a market orientation, but how to support 'diverse institutions that ensure markets enhance people's freedom and human security as effectively as possible'.[1] Thus, along with an increase in financial prosperity should be development of public services in the health and education sector, as well as a proper distribution of resources and equitable development outcomes.[2] This in turn relates not only to health and education, since a healthy and educated population further supports and sustains proper market growth, but is also linked to adequate food and water. Similarly, other issues like matters concerning

1 United Nations Commission on Human Security (2003), 'Human Security Now' www.humansecurity-chs.org/finalreport/index.html at 75.

2 United Nations Commission on Human Security (2003), at 76.

the environment come to the fore since degradation of natural resources (such as heavy logging for fossil fuels) erodes the ecology, thereby leading to long-term food security issues.[3] Ignoring a sustainable development program or refusal to uphold some form of balance between human security and the environment further tends to deepen rural poverty given the latter's historical reliance on land and resources for sustenance.[4] The result can very well be a bottoming out of the market. Taking the problem a step further, while terrorism is not limited to poverty stricken areas (indeed, its backers might be quite wealthy), terrorist organizations take advantage of the poor upon recognizing that 'despair creates favourable conditions for terrorist projects and actions'.[5]

In this chapter, the aim is to consider the underlying advantage in referring to human security as a possible paradigm, as well as account for its potential role within the international framework. Human security is by no means a panacea for addressing the ills of the international system. Indeed, one of its central detriments is its somewhat malleable and amorphous 'normative' structure. Nonetheless, human security can be the means by which to force states to account for issues of people and proper development, notions that have been difficult to effectively incorporate into the current international context. Further, the amorphous nature of the human security concept can serve it well when considered from a transformative approach since the goal need not be the creation of a norm per se but rather the delineation of factors that merit consideration by the international system when accounting for the security of people, groups and individuals. That is, human security can bridge a diverse set of subjects, not necessarily to attain a determinant normative standard, but to direct states and international organizations in making decisions and policy choices. Thus the purpose of this chapter is to consider the merits of why and how reference is made to human security, and account for possible avenues by which it might operate.

Contrasting Human Security

The goal of human security is not solely order and stability, a common goal of states in general, but also justice and emancipation that would ensure a

3 United Nations Commission on Human Security (2003), at 16.
4 United Nations Commission on Human Security (2003), at 17.
5 United Nations Commission on Human Security (2003), at 74.

functioning existence.[6] It is the attempt to connect the security of people with the overall security of the society.[7] Traditional approaches to security are state centric, focusing on military threats or (in a neo-realist context) on economic threats to the state.[8] Such an understanding of security is rather narrow as it ignores other aspects of security that are needed to properly create and implement an effective policy that provides actual security for the population being protected.

Basing security on military needs is essentially rooted in territorial notions that do not fully translate into security for one's citizens as such. Recognising the shift in global politics indicates aspects beyond military threats and an accounting of economic stability, quality of life, human rights and the environment, along with migration patterns and internal ethnic conflicts.[9] If security of the state in the overall is the central driving factor, then other factors also should enter the equation of security such as preventing civilian unrest due to famine, providing a context for sustainable development, or creating a viable program to eliminate illiteracy.[10] These policy decisions have just as profound an effect on the state and its security goals as would a military threat, albeit they also can emanate from internal threats to security. This is especially the case in a post-cold war scenario where the previous grounds for security, such as a deterrence policy, has actually caused greater insecurity, particularly with the spread of nuclear capacity to a greater number of states.[11] There is a need for a people-

---

6 Acharya, A. (2001), 'Human Security: East Versus West', 56 *International Journal* 442–460.

7 Lodgaard, S. (2000), 'Human Security: Concept and Operationalization', available at: http://www.hsph.%20harvard.edu/hpcr/events/hsworkshop/lodgaard.pdf. The paper also has been published in a more elaborate form as Chapter 2 in Muller, M. and de gaay Fortman, B. (eds), (2004), *From Warfare to Welfare: Human Security in a Southern African Context* (Assen, Royal van Gorcum).

8 Wilkin. P. (1999), 'Human Security and Class in a Global Economy', 23–33 in Thomas, C. and Wilkin P. (eds), *Globalisation, Human Security and the African Experience* (L. Reinner Pub., USA).

9 Axworthy, L. (2004), 'Human Security: An Opening for UN Reform', 245–260 in Price, R. and Zacher, M. (eds), *The United Nations and Global Security* (Palgrave, Macmillan, NY); Newman, D. (2000), 'A Human Security Council? Applying a "Human Security" Agenda to Security Council Reform', 31 *Ottawa L. Rev.* 213.

10 Acharya (2001).

11 Jones, R. (1999), *Security Strategy and Critical Theory* (L. Reinner Pub., USA).

centred approach that incorporates a global perspective of security.[12] The point is that upon considering the 'security' aspect of human security, the idea is to promote reassurance, and not solely deterrence, by considering for example military security along with other avenues that guarantee a proper human existence such as environmental concerns[13] or ecological preservation.

Human security combines issues of traditional state oriented security into a present-day context that strives for non-military threats (freedom from fear – a negative application) as well as issues of development (freedom from want – a positive aspect). For example, the UNDP focused on aspects of human security that called for a universal approach whose components are interdependent yet upholds security via prevention and is people-centred.[14] The key categories that demanded some form of human security approach were economics, food, health, environment, along with personal, community and political aspects.

Even further, moving away from a state-centric approach towards people oriented goals turns one towards issues involving human rights, and acknowledges this overlap between human rights and human security concerns. Although not serving to conflict between the two, human security can begin to address many of the inherent problems within the human rights system, while also allowing for the application of human rights. Thus, human rights can be enhanced by a paradigm that considers security aspects from both a freedom from fear as well as want perspective, away from the context of state to individual relationship. This eliminates the overbearing and at times diminishing needs of the state that might not always maintain an interest in the desired ends. Human rights are opened up to additional considerations and evaluations pursuant to a human security paradigm that combines needs and dignity in a seamless fashion

12 King, G. and Murray, C. (2001), 'Rethinking Human Security', 116 *Political Science Quarterly* 585–610.

13 *See* e.g. Murphy, M (1999), 'Achieving Economic Security with Swords as Ploughshares: The Modern Use of Force to Combat Environmental Degradation', 39 *Va, J, Intl. L.* 1181 noting the importance of treating environmental issues as matters of security (asserting that it would fall under an issue of self defence and can serve as grounds for humanitarian intervention); Tinker, C. (1992), '"Environmental Security" in the United Nations: Not a Matter for the Security Council', 59 *Tenn. L. Rev.* 787 (linking environmental protection with traditional notions of state security).

14 King and Murray (2001–02), at 589 referring to the United Nations Development Program.

and as a unit, rather than as competing or contrasting goods.[15] Similarly, one can begin to account for development needs away from the glare of state security by invoking other forms of balancing and interests that the state might not be able to consider or, in the realist context, even desire to consider in a consequentialist framework (as linked to immediate state interests).

Additionally, given that human security combines aspects of state security with growth and development, there is no sense of correlative duties as found within the human rights system but rather a notion of achieving a specific objective as the means for attaining the desired end(s). Human security incorporates aspects relating to the human condition that go beyond entitlements, including for example matters like controlling small arms.[16] The capacity to achieve some form of human security can begin to be addressed via multilateral dialogue and cooperative actions pursuant to an existing framework, as proposed by the demands of the human security paradigm. Thus, human security sidesteps the oft used excuse of discretion or necessity as grounds for suppressing human rights.

While the West has focused on freedom from fear, especially when considering problems of terrorism and attacks on civilians from informal groups, the notion of human security is to integrate the problems faced by individuals (freedom from fear) along with those of communities (freedom from want) to create a more effective model for addressing issues such as terrorism or the environment, especially given the broader realization being asserted. Human security acts to secure some form of social protection against risks or external threats (to address fears) as a means of ensuring the implementation of programs that provide for the people (to address wants).

Given that human security proposes to bridge the needs of population groups with the desire to uphold the dignity of individuals, an advantage then is the manner in which it incorporates aspects of the development process. Human security is both a communal and individual understanding

15 *Cf.* Saul, B. (2006), 'The Dangers of the United Nations' "New Security Agenda": "Human Security" in the Asia-Pacific Region', 1 *Asian J. Comp. L.* 1 who asserts that human security can dilute the normative inroads that human rights has attained. While this tends to accord a somewhat lofty position to human rights (one that is not always supported by state practice), it also does not allow for consideration of the various pratfalls of the human rights system, especially in the relativist context or when considering matters like development.

16 *See* United Nations Commission on Human Security (2003).

of human rights. No longer must the human rights process be rooted solely in an atomist framework, thereby making it difficult to conceive of rights or some form of entitlements in a group context, because human security can allow for consideration of communal groups that are deprived of certain fundamental necessities. Human security allows for the realization that social and individual protections are inter-linked, such as to begin to remove problems of relativism since the focus shifts to localized notions and courses of action based on social development and the needs of the local peoples (at least as a means of enhancing opportunities and capabilities).[17] Additionally, human security is understood as emanating from the perceptions and vital needs of the target population, thus creating a dynamic notion that is not locked in to a particular conceptual framework.[18]

Within the human security context, the centrality of the state is not the focus but rather the importance of providing security for specific population groups. The notion of state discretion as such is thereby qualified. The same can be said for social and economic rights, where state discretion reigns supreme due to the acknowledgement of progressive realization pursuant to the means and capacities of the state.[19] Yet, human security moves one away from the state as the central character towards a recognition of the individuals and groups that are asserting specific needs for their very existence.

This is a rather important step for the international system as it opens up vistas for expanding upon human rights protection as well as addressing many of the inherent shortcomings identified by developing states and other groups that have not always attained recognition or have been part of the formalized human rights process. There exist many instances whereby human rights protection as such is either unattainable or simply non-applicable given the lack of any unitary overlying power or controlling authority.

---

17 Michael, S. (2002), 'The Role of NGOs in Human Security', Hauser Center for Nonprofit Organizations, Working Paper No. 12 available at: http://ssrn.com/abstractid=351240.

18 Alkire, S. (2003), 'Concepts of Human Security', in Chen, L., Fukuda-Parr, S., and Seidensticker, S. (eds), *Human Insecurity in a Globalised World* (Harvard University Press, USA) (noting the multi-directional aspects of human security and the problems of vagueness due to the open-ended nature of the concept).

19 Seidensticker, E. (2002), 'Human Security, Human Rights and Human Development', available at: http://www.humansecurity-chs.org/activities/outreach/0206harvard.pdf.

For example, a notion of shared sovereignty for an autonomous region[20] raises the question over human rights protection and overall responsibilities of the emerging power. How is an emerging sovereign to maintain human rights protection, especially if the sovereign is not fully entrenched or defined? Can human rights provide policy guidelines in a shared sovereign situation where a formal state–individual framework is non-existent? With a focus on human security, it is understood that in a shared sovereignty, the goal is to provide for population security in a manner that allows for sustainable growth and development. Human security provides a framework and goals for autonomous regions or emerging states even if human rights might have to be suspended or cannot be implemented,[21] particularly concerning policy goals for an emerging entity and guidelines for international assistance beyond solely human rights protection for individuals located therein.

The expanding vista of human security is also quite apparent for other aspects of international law that demand some form of normative relationship between systems, such as incorporating notions of human security into the context of humanitarian norms. Human security can begin to address a variety of normative gaps in the international system found in humanitarian norms where there is a great difficulty in accounting for non-state actors engaged in conflicts as well as adapting the norms to internal conflicts, essentially the prevalent forum in most present conflict situations. Alternative approaches to security are mandated by the issues confronting states in conflict given problems like intrastate warfare, the link between violent conflict and economic underdevelopment, targeting of civilians in internal conflicts, and the use of child soldiers. Addressing these issues requires an alternative perception outside of traditional competing ideologies and alliance systems.[22] Human security can provide the wherewithal for incorporating aspects of policy decisions and direction where the state apparatus is either nonexistent or too weak to operate. Even more so in instances where the state is dominant over other groups, acting to suppress basic rights in the interest of state security.

---

20 *See* e.g. Krasner, S. (2003), 'The Hole in the Whole: Sovereignty, Shared Sovereignty, and International Law', 25 *Mich. J Intl. L.* 1075.

21 Fox, G.and Nolte, G (2002), 'Intolerant Democracies', 36 *Harv. Intl. L.J. 1.*

22 Axworthy, L. (2004), at 253–254. *See also* Belz, D (2005), 'Is International Humanitarian Law Lapsing into Irrelevance in the War on International Terror?', (Tel-Aviv University Law Faculty Papers) http://law.bepress.com/cgi/viewcontent.cgi?article=1023&context=taulwps regarding humanitarian norms and terrorism, given the inadequacy of current approaches towards humanitarian norms as ineffective tools for addressing the problems associated with terrorism.

It has been noted that there is grave difficulty for states to implement humanitarian norms within internal armed conflicts. With a rise to the threat of civilians, there are many instances where the state as such does not exist and the threat to the population derives from an unrecognised actor, thereby leaving civilians as helpless targets outside the protection of the international community.[23]

The oft-cited common article 3 of the Geneva Conventions that is to presumably protect non-combat personnel in internal conflict is a rather vague and general article addressing military violations that are not wholly applicable to all forms of post conflict relationships between the military and civilians.[24] Whilst the 1977 Additional Protocols II expanded upon Article 3, and interpretation of the article has progressed via other international bodies such as the Former Yugoslavia tribunal in The Hague,[25] the focus again has been on the form of military conduct and those who should not be attacked. Additionally, interpretations to be garnered for this article, such as the statute of the international criminal court, indicate that the focus is on grave breaches of military violations, such as rape or treacherous killings.[26] There are a host of related issues to be addressed, be it an international or non-international form of conflict, for a distressed population group that are not adequately considered by the international system.[27]

While some have asserted that normative gaps in humanitarian norms can be addressed by reference to international human rights,[28] such an assertion is based on the assumption that a state exists in such areas

23 Bruderlein, C.(2001), 'People's Security as a New Means of Global Stability', 83 *Intl. Rev. Red Cross* 353–366.

24 Crillo-Suarez, A. (1999), 'Hors de Logique: Contemporary Issues in International Humanitarian Law as Applied to Internal Armed Conflict', 15 *Am. U Intl. Rev 1* (emphasizing the importance of the interplay between legal and non-legal forces as a means of further development).

25 Byron, C. (2001), 'Armed Conflicts: International or Non-International?', 6 *J Conflict Studies* 63 (discussing the approaches of the Yugoslav tribunal towards humanitarian norms as applied to internal conflict).

26 *See* e.g. Byron, C. (2001).

27 Robinson, D. and Oosterveld, V. (2001), 'The Evolution of International Humanitarian Law', 161–170 in McRae, R. ands Hubert, D. (eds), *Human Security and the New Diplomacy: Protecting People, Promoting Peace* (McGill-Queens University Press, Montreal) (noting the need for greater compliance of humanitarian norms in all forms of conflicts as one way to promote human security).

28 *See* e.g. Meron, T. (2000), 'The Humanization of Humanitarian Law', 94 *Am. J. Intl. L.* 239–278.

when oftentimes it does not (or at least, does not adequately control the area).[29] The structural problems are further entrenched when recognizing that human rights were based specifically upon a relationship between an individual and the state, hence the very notion of a rights-duty form of relationship implies the existence of an authoritative or controlling entity. While human rights for example might be deemed to apply on a state controlling a territory,[30] the operation and application of human rights is unclear and rather unsteady upon factoring in the military aspects involved for an occupation force and the potential lack of formalized relations between the military and the population under its control.[31]

Designation of the conflict is also an issue, such as the difficulty in deciding whether or not a conflict is internal (an important aspect due to the different standards implicated in the Geneva Conventions and one that has been demanded from the humanitarian norm framework) along with the application of standards to non-traditional groups like rebel factions.[32] Further, the context in which these systems operate do not always allow for prevention since humanitarian norms are geared towards the manner in which to address situations of conflict, while human rights tend to be reactive to violations.

Human security has been cited as a means by which to address some of the shortcomings inherent in humanitarian norms. The key reason for

---

The International Court of Justice implicitly assumed that human rights are to inform humanitarian norms in the Advisory Opinion concerning the Israeli separation fence. *See* ICJ Advisory Opinion Legal Consequences of the Construction of a Wall in the Occupied Palestinian Territory decided 9/7/04 at para. 106.

29 Shoham, U (1996), 'The Principle of Legality and the Israeli Military Government in the Territories', 153 *Mil. L. Rev.* 245 (outlining the problems confronted by the Israeli military in the Occupied Territories due to the necessity for a functioning rule of law given the long duration of the occupation)

30 *See* e.g. Human Rights Committee, General Comment Number 31 at paragraph 10.

31 Watkin, K. (2004), 'Controlling the Use of Force: A Role for Human Rights Norms in Contemporary Armed Conflict', 98 *Am. J. Intl. L.* 1–34 noting the problems in integrating human rights and humanitarian norms, and calling for a measured approach that accounts for the security needs of the military as well as the population under its control.

32 Ball, D (2004), 'Toss the Travaux? Application of the Fourth Geneva Convention to the Middle East Conflict – A Modern (Re)Assessment', 79 *N. Y. U. L. Rev.* 990 (noting how the Geneva Conventions were not intended to apply to a situation of long-term occupation).

this capacity is that security is not state centred or linked to the traditional dichotomy of military power and civilian needs. Thus, security is not meant to be understood in the realist sense as solely preserving military stability or averting military threats. Indeed, part of the problem with a focus on such a form of security is linked to the idea that what is good for the state is good for the society under its protection. Yet, in a realist context, it is apparent that this notion of security is too abstract as the state is acting for its interests along with the social forces that reflect those interests, but not necessarily to always benefit the overall social interests or the individuals under their control.[33] For example, securing food as a means of preventing unrest might not fall under the purview of state security as understood thus far. By contrast, environmental or ecological protection as grounds for security ensures for food production and developing an economic focus on internal threats and the needs of the population, thereby shifting from military security towards one that addresses the actual problems confronting the population at large.[34]

Why Human Security

While the aforementioned is significant in that human security can assist in addressing some normative issues for international law, it is also important to factor in structural changes in the international system that move one towards reassessment and towards developing a role for human security. As noted *supra*, human security can be a legitimating element for the state. That is, security of the people overall coupled with a notion of societal security not only leads to human security but also legitimacy for a state. The state is not acting solely for the benefit of its existence, but also for the improvement of the individuals (citizens and others) who fall within the state's purview. This is a rather important aspect when accounting for the changes and shifts that have occurred to state sovereignty, particularly

33 Wilkin (1999). *Compare* Liotta, P. (2002), 'Boomerang Effect: The Convergence of National and Human Security', 33 *Security Dialogue* 473–488 (noting the need for a proper balance between the traditional security needs of the state and reference to the human security needs of a population at large) *with* Grayson, K. (2003), 'Securitization and the Boomerang Debate: A Rejoinder to Liotta and Smith-Windsor', 34 *Security Dialogue* 337–343 (noting the importance of preserving human security as its own ethos, especially to preserve its underlying benefits and afforded protections outside of a military context).

34 The World Bank similarly does not limit its understanding of security solely to economic issues, as it also incorporates conflict prevention and resolution as essential end-goals. Alkire (2003) at 28.

with the movement away from an international system that places the state at the centre of the apparatus.

What can be gleaned is that the state is not the sole addressee for providing security to its citizens. Granted that in a *realpolitik* context the state is the key actor, yet such an approach is being countered by other forms of reality as indicated by the role of the media (and the general public) as an influencing factor, non-governmental organizations,[35] and reference to international standards that also tend to influence and even alter the position of states.[36] Privatisation efforts of states indicate a lesser role in the realm of public services as well as a form of deference to other external bodies in carrying out such roles. Similarly, acknowledging minority rights and other groups like indigenous peoples concerning their standing and interests in land or other forms of autonomy both in the domestic and international plane creates a change in the position of the state and the role that it plays concerning the security of its inhabitants and as the overall representative of their interests. The sovereign state as such is characterized by forces that are many times external to its control, including the foundations in law (such as the governmental structure) since the elements materialize via many factors that shape and influence the sovereign state, such as economic interests.[37] Additional changes indicating an altered status are the approach towards crimes against humanity and genocide as universal prohibitions and matters of international concern, an emerging obligation of states to utilize humanitarian intervention, and the growth of transnational migration particularly among the labour force.[38]

---

35 Cullen, H. and Morrow, K. (2001), 'International civil society in international law: The growth of NGO participation', 1 *Non-State Actors and Intl. L.* 7–39 (referring to the influential role of non-governmental organisations within international law).

36 *See* e.g. Reinicke, W. and Witte, J. (2000), 'Interdependence, Globalization, and Sovereignty: The Role of Non-binding International Legal Accords', 75–100 in Shelton, D. (ed.), *Commitment and Compliance: The Role of Non-Binding Norms in the International Legal System* (Oxford University Press, UK) noting that globalization for example created a qualitative change to the international system, given the expanded role of private actors, new technologies, and global corporate networks, all of which challenge the state's operational role as a sovereign.

37 *See* e.g. Saunders, L. (2001), 'Rich and Rare are the Gems they War: Holding De Beers Accountable for Trading Conflict Diamonds', 24 *Fordham Intl. L. J.* 1402 (asserting that multi-national corporations play an extensive role in shaping policy and preventing human rights abuses).

38 *See* e.g. Benhabib, S. (2005), 'On the Alleged Conflict between Democracy and International Law', 19 *Ethics and Intl. Affairs* 85–101.

The state is principally a territorial unit, whereby the population group within this territory serves as instrumentalities to further the interests and goals of the state. Human security moves one away from a territorial centred understanding that dominated notions of security in the 19th and 20th centuries towards an emphasis on human beings and human development.[39] Thus, one can discern both a qualitative and quantitative move away from the state to the basic needs of localized groups or at least local specifications as demanded by the situation (rather than a Western orientation of pre-conceived necessities for individuals).[40] As such, human security calls for an approach that focuses on institutional protection as a responsive and preventative policy, and not an episodic and reactive attempt to retroactively protect people in need or at peril.[41]

Unlike the domestic arena where the social-state connection might be more readily apparent, on the international front, the state is acting for specific interests that might not always incorporate social benefits given the link of security to traditional power interests of the state (such as military needs at the expense of necessary social development).[42] Similarly, human security shifts attention to a more localized framework and to local specificities of particular groups.[43] The knowledge and eventual exercise of power by local groups addresses aspects like unfair distribution and desire for basic and material needs.

Human Security and an Alternative Approach

The turn of human security to other aspects of state relationships and responsibilities is clearly a fluid concept focusing on prevention (similar to state security) but one that attempts to incorporate surrounding aspects influencing the state and its policy choices. Similar to the current international system and unlike a state-centric approach, human security

39 Alkire, S. (2002), 'Conceptual Framework for Human Security', available at: http://www.humansecurity-chs.org/activities/outreach/frame.pdf at 2–3.

40 Thomas, C. (1999), 'Introduction', 1 in Thomas, C. and Wilkin P. (eds), *Globalisation, Human Security and the African Experience* (L. Reinner Pub., USA); Wolf, A. (1999), 'Water and Human Security', 3 AVISO: An Information Bulletin on Global Environmental Change and Human Security available at: http://www.peacemagazine.org/9910/wurfel.htm (making a similar claim regarding water and security).

41 Alkire (2002).

42 Wilkin (1999).

43 Thomas (1999).

welcomes a multilateral structure.[44] Thus upon recognizing the changes to traditional sovereignty whereby territorial recognition and non-intervention into domestic affairs are not the sole determinant factors for imposing international norms, one can begin to conceive of different approaches to security. Human security is a process-based notion incorporating various non-state actors into the international framework and relying on multiple levels of governance beyond the international-domestic dichotomy.[45] Human security then is an example of transnational governance that can serve as a response to the shortcomings of traditional notions of security in a manner that adequately accounts for change.

Perceiving human security as a process readily adapts to the approach of Foucault, especially concerning the envisioned relationship between the population at large and the state's role in providing security. Granted the apparent aspects of power are inherent here given the multiplicity of actors involved in the process and the various roles and influences that each may have on the functions and policies of the other.[46] However there is more at stake since human security relates as well to the condition of liberty. That is, liberty is linked to a condition of security and the mechanisms relevant to upholding such security. Security, as understood by Foucault, is not a broad element of political power to be exercised by the state, but a principle of political method and practice capable of various modes of combination with other principles and practices within the diverse governmental configuration.[47] Unlike sovereignty that focuses on notions of territory and space, or even modes of discipline (such as the rule of law) to be exercised between the state and the individual, security can be understood as dealing with the ensemble of the population. Security then need not be implemented as a form of control, but as a recoding of the political order.

Human security is not centred on ideas of control as such, but on calculations of the possible and probable, thereby altering the relationship with the sovereign state from one of function to that of transaction. The state of course plays a role but it is understood as not being the sole unit

---

44 Axworthy (2004).

45 Axworthy (2004); Thomas, N. and Tow, E. (2002), 'The Utility of Human Security: Sovereignty and Humanitarian Intervention', 33 *Security Dialogue* 177–192.

46 *See* discussion *supra* at Chapter 2.

47 Gordon, C. (1991), 'Governmental Rationality: An Introduction', 1–53 in Burchell, G., Gordon, C., and Miller, P. (eds), *The Foucault Effect: Studies in Governmentality* (University of Chicago Press, USA).

for action and for effecting change. Such transactions incorporate a host of activity relevant to the status and position of population groups and individuals that transcend the role of the state and allow for recognition of other actors as well. Civil society for example plays an important role in the common interplay of power (in an ongoing sense) allowing for a prominent function of various non-state actors and international organizations to assist and direct with the development of policy and overall human security.[48] The relationship with the state then is in the isomorphic sense, whereby an intimate symbiosis is created between the state and its apparatus, and the population groups found therein in a manner that recognises their position and allows for all relevant actors to voice an opinion and influence policy.[49] Furthermore, the focus on the welfare of the population in a broad sense reflects Foucault's notion of bio-politics, which shifted attention away from the state as the central figure towards issues that are central to the human security framework.[50] Thus, the area in which the human dwells is the focus, with the task falling on the government, international organisations, non-governmental organisations and the populace at large to become active producers within the overall political system.

What results from such an approach is a leaning towards a transformative understanding since the goal is to conceptualise an environment for operation in a constitutive sense, and not solely function via administrative procedures as pre-determined by the state.[51] The process itself becomes the focal point without any need for a formalised, pre-supposed, normative framework.[52] Rather, what emerges is an allowance for all relevant actors to play a part in shaping and defining human security as needed and determined by particular conditions.[53] A transformative approach then conforms nicely to allow for a conceptualization of human security in a manner that need not rely upon existing normative systems but rather allow for human security to develop in a descriptive sense, as the needs

48 *See* discussion *infra* at Chapter 7.

49 Jones (1999), at Chapter 4.

50 Lipschutz, R. (2005), 'Global civil society and global governmentality: Resistance, reform or resignation?' 171 in Baker, G. and Chandler, D. (eds), *Global Civil Society: Contested Futures* (Routledge, UK).

51 King and Murray (2001); Newman (2000).

52 Paris, R. (2001), 'Human Security: Paradigm Shift or Hot Air?', 26 *Intl. Sec.* 87–102.

53 *Compare* Suhrke, A. (1999), 'Human Security and the Interests of States', 30 *Security Dialogue* 265–276 (noting the need for a conceptual clarification of human security that adequately identifies the goals of human security).

of populations or groups shift and sway depending on necessities and surrounding changes.

Indeed, it is the lack of a normative framework that allows for the development of human security as an immediate answer to the particular needs of various population groups as well as the international system at large. Describing human security as incorporating downward trends between the state and different groups and individuals, upward trends between the state and the international system (such as for environmental issues), horizontal directions depending on the specific problems of a particular population group, and the multi-directional focus on all aspects of governance (including local, national, and international)[54] points to a transformative context that is not seeking a final measure but is allowing for the existence of a relative and sliding standard.

Human security also reflects the shift in the understanding of power within the international system, particularly away from the state. Human security opens the door for the international system to account for other actors not necessarily as replacing the state, but to provide a descriptive context of consideration in which other actors also play a key role. Non-state actors become active participants in the political paradigm formerly inhabited by the state by broadening the meaning and implication of security to incorporate factors that continue to receive the attention of the international system, with a view towards creating an effective solution. Human security in that sense is acknowledging the Foucauldian approach to power given the potential impact of a variety of actors to shape policies and create initiatives for groups and individuals, where the proposals emanate from outside a formalised state structure and yet have resonance and meaning in the international context. While human security on a conceptual level might be vague or arbitrary, the underlying goal is not the creation of norms, but rather to allow for the development of a framework that addresses the interests of a complex and inter-linked international system.

Conclusion

Understanding governmentality according to Foucault is to perceive the state as a function of changes in practice, and not necessarily the development of institutions as such.[55] A transformative approach to the state then is not

54 *See* e.g. Alkire (2003), at 20.

55 Gordon (1991).

to approach the state as the final arbiter of security, but rather to delineate state action and the various political factors attendant thereto as operating in combination with other configurations and processes, both internal (such as a local government or indigenous group) and external (such as an international organization or non-governmental organisations).

Human security need not supplant the state, but it does call for a broader form approach that tends to the immediate needs of population groups and address international matters, whereby the measure for concern and the programs initiated do not solely derive from state action and their particular interests. Rather, the relation with the state is on a transactional level, with human security serving as a platform to express and entrench the positions of various international and domestic actors. Thus, the inherent open-ended nature of human security actually tends to enhance its capacity given the complex international issues that intermingle with a variety of social issues. Human security provides a paradigmatic context for operation and opens the door for further development and protection both via the existing means (to incorporate a host of different actors) as well as meeting the desired ends.

Chapter 7

Non-Governmental Organizations and Power

Introduction

The previous two chapters on human rights and human security demonstrate changing patterns within the international legal framework that have not been adequately accounted for in a structural sense when considering a state-centric approach to international law. Human rights clearly elevated the role of the individual, and eventually the group, along with other actors such as non-governmental organizations, who represent non-state interests.[1] Human security proposes a broader incorporative international framework given the intermingling of issues and approaches within the world today and the need for a more expanded and inclusive understanding of relevant actors and interests. Clearly these developments merit a further evaluation regarding the shifting positions of the variety of international actors, their inter-relationships and standing, and the effect that it has on the position of the state and the manner of international relations. Additionally, given the incorporation of actors other than states who maintain an operative and at times influential role, it is important to consider the overlying international framework that has undergone a shift in focus, and begin to account for the manner by which international relations occur and international law evolves within this broader context.

Part of the problem noted with human rights is that even with a focus on the individual as a subject, the understanding and scope of the right is still defined by pre-conceived notions that entrench governmental perceptions and impose institutional constraints. Thus, human rights are ingrained with problems like relativism since the claim to a "higher" notion of human capacity and treatment is based on pre-defined ideals and linked to inherent cultural implications. The chapter on human rights then sought to transgress such an approach towards human rights by understanding the assertions of a right as taking place within a discursive field, as a means of understanding the actors' various positions and their

1 *See* discussion *infra.*

underlying derivations for making claims. This in turn creates a material effect on the manner of practice because understanding the discourse (as reflecting knowledge and thought) leads to an accounting of the various techniques and perceptions that are part of the arena of ideas. As ideas become part of these permutations of power (via discourse and counter-discourses), liberty is further promoted since the potential for promoting resistance to another's ideas or asserting one's views is possible given the variety of actors involved in the power process.[2] The result is that power also is a constituting process, not solely regressive and confining, such that it allows for an ongoing agonistic relationship between the participating actors, rather than the solidification of power into strategic dominations.

A similar analysis will be referred to in this chapter, albeit within the framework of the international process itself that engages both state and non-state actors when considered from the context of global civil society. Given the approach to power as moving beyond subjection towards one that also produces a certain form of ordering within society, attention will turn towards the notion of global civil society with a specific analysis of the role of non-governmental organizations in the greater international framework. Non-governmental organizations personify the overall notion of global civil society, encompassing the goals of enhanced individual participation and an enlarged political community, and indicating the resultant changes that have occurred to the international system. Aspects pertaining to the compelling influence of non-governmental organizations on local initiatives, state decisions, as well as within the confines of international organizations, indicate that non-governmental organizations play an important role within the international system. They maintain rather strong capacity for action and influence, both on the state as well as within various international bodies, and are playing an active function within international discourse to implement some form of change and provide for the assertion of a variety of views not always considered by the state.

Recognising the role of the non-governmental organisation as a typical non-state international actor, there also have been a number of recent critical evaluations of non-governmental organizations, usually relating to both internal and external structural problems concerning their manner of operation and approaches towards specific issues. Specifically, the noted problems relate to the standing and sources of influence for non-governmental organizations, along with a call for some form of internal

2 Simons, J. (1995), *Foucault and the Political* (Routledge, UK) at 56.

accountability to their represented interests and external accountability to the formation of policy and goals.

The proposed approach will involve a turn towards the Foucauldian framework as a means of considering and assessing the changes within the international system. The goal is to demonstrate how the global civil society process, and non-governmental organizations as a typical actor therein, in essence reflect the power/knowledge relationship proposed by Foucault. Providing a referential context, given that the global civil society actors' interactions reflect Foucault's explication of power and knowledge, one can begin to address the criticisms levelled at non-governmental organizations to conceive an operable form of global governance that on the one hand maintains the benefits of having a disparate group of actors without conceding an overly important role to such actors given the strive to comprehend positions and constantly examine (and re-examine) the proposed limitations.

Global Civil Society Generally

Global civil society emerged as a third realm to account for the assertion of additional interests outside the state or international organizations and to enhance participation of such actors, becoming an integral part of the ongoing power process in the international framework. Global civil society is in essence public interest actors outside the government or state who are not solely pursuing market-oriented economic benefits or particular state interests. Such actors operate between the realm of the family and the state, with a view towards contributing to policy making and law creation that accounts for the host of interests affected by domestic and international decisions.[3]

Global civil society appeals to a broad array of actors within the international realm. Development theorists and those with a liberal orientation appreciate civil society for its grassroots approach to social change and that it serves as a key building block for democracy. Economic and market oriented actors value global civil society since it plays an important role in furthering deregulation of the state and promoting privatisation, especially via self help initiatives that lead to lower governmental involvement and increased market efficiency. Further, those

3 Leigh, I. (2004), 'Civil Society, Democracy, and the Law', Geneva Centre for the Democratic Control of Armed Forces, Working Paper # 130 available at: http://www.dcaf.ch/_docs/WP130.pdf.

with a more socialist orientation welcome global civil society due to its inherent link to social organizations and support for social governance via the group and the greater community.[4]

Global civil society began to re-emerge as an important issue for consideration following a variety of post-Cold War changes, one principal factor being the ongoing globalisation of markets. As markets became more intertwined and technological innovations began to take root in a number of key consumer industries, institutions overall were subject to different pressures, leading to a call for heightened international regulation as well as pressure from states to provide for oversight. The emerging multi-layered governance led to market regulation from both domestic and international sources as well as, in certain instances, greater privatisation.[5] Coupled with this was a prominent role for other actors within international markets like multi-national corporations who continued to spread their web of influence as markets became broader and more dispersed throughout the world.[6] The necessity then arose for representing the variety of interests not adequately encompassed within the state/market divide, such as to incorporate the host of interests affected by state decisions that might be ignored by states (like minority positions) as well as those not properly considered within a market framework (such as environmental effects).[7] Thus, globalisation led to the denationalisation of a variety of what had previously been exclusive state activities not only within the market, but also within political and social contexts as well.

The large debt of lesser developed countries during the eighties and nineties and the need for services previously provided by the socialist states during the post-Cold War period also assisted with the enhanced role of global civil society. Less public spending and a stronger focus on the private sector as the provider of services opened the door for greater

4 Stiles, K. (2000), 'Grassroots Empowerment: States, non-state actors and global policy formulation', in Higgott, R., Underhill, G., and Bieler, A. (eds) *Non-State Actors and Authority in the Global System* (Routledge, UK) at 33.

5 *See* generally Scholte, J. (2000), *Globalization: A Critical Introduction* (Palgrave, UK).

6 Kenny, M. and Germain, R (2005), 'The idea(l) of global civil society', in Germain, R. and Kenny, M. (eds), *The Idea of Global Civil Society: Politics and Ethics in a Globalizing Era* (Routledge, UK).

7 Chandhoke, N. (2002), 'Limits of Global Civil Society', in Glasius, M., Kaldor, M. and Anheier, H. (eds), *Global Civil Society* (Centre for the Study of Global Civil Society, UK) available at: http://www.lse.ac.uk/Depts/global/yearbook02chapters.htm.

engagement by civil society actors. Another result of this was a liberalist leaning in the monetary aid provided to civil society actors given the source of funds being principally from the West, and the agenda of global civil society being established by states or international agencies with a particular desired focus, such as the World Health Organisation focusing on strategies for specific health issues like the AIDs virus.[8]

Recognising these developments, a number of key goals for the variety of global civil society actors have been identified. One is the natural extension of the political community beyond the state to include non-state actors outside the realm of international organizations or international institutions.[9] The understood goal is to not only to enhance participation of non-state actors, but also to construct a more "ethically aware" political community that accounts for a wider variety of interests other than state interests or those of the global market.[10] Another is to emphasise human agency as being a viable political consideration beyond economic determinism.[11] In this context, the realist conception of international relations is not only a reflection of division and conflict between states, but also is responsible for producing the framework, leading to a reproduced form of international structure that inherently will account for other interests.[12] Furthermore, the emergence of global civil society has been understood as extending democracy beyond the confines of the state, whereby the international space is expanded to include a variety of self-help organizations that operate outside of formal political circles.[13]

The move away from post-Cold War cosmopolitanism towards recognising cultural differences and emphasising economic development and the rule of law as an engine for change and improvement has also caused problems of wealth disparity and assertions of relative perceptions

---

8 Stiles (2000), at 37–41 noting the downside to the external control via funding was less of a focus on grassroots issues as determined by local actors in the field.

9 Chandler, D. (2005), *Constructing Global Civil Society: Morality and Power in International Relations* (Palgrave Macmillan, UK).

10 Baker, G. and Chandler, D. (2005), 'Introduction: global civil society and the future of world politics', in Baker, G. and Chandler, D. (eds), *Global Civil Society: Contested Futures* (Routledge, UK). Of course, this notion of injecting morality into the international framework is problematic given the variety of interests at stake and the possibility for a broad array of actors with pre-conceived notions and desired ends. *See* discussion *infra.*

11 Baker and Chandler (2005).

12 Chandler (2005).

13 Baker and Chandler (2005).

regarding the social construct (rather than simply relying upon problematic universalist notions).[14] International actors along with local groups linked to for example ethnic, cultural, or religious identities (to name but a few) recognise their position and local conditions as inherently relevant and defining, such as to move away from a universal doctrine. What has resulted however is that a variety of non-state public organizations, especially non-governmental organizations, have begun to play a rather active role within the global civil society framework due to the scope of their operations, the broad format of their fieldwork, and the ability to infuse the international process with greater transparency.

With greater communication capabilities due to significant technological innovations, and the claim to moral legitimacy on the basis of representing public opinion of a variety of groups, non-governmental organizations have risen as important actors in the international framework.[15] The need for some form of governance and oversight over the globalised free market, even within various international bodies that have served to regulate international markets like the World Trade Organisation, have tended to reference non-governmental organizations as a means of rounding-out their decisions and ensuring for access to all forms of information.[16] Non-governmental organizations also have become more assertive in the development of international documents, participating in the monitoring and implementation of norms and engaging the variety of existing dispute resolution processes.[17] Thus, non-governmental organizations are

14 Gamble, A. and Kenny. M. (2005), 'Ideological contestation, transnational civil society, and global politics', in Germain, R. and Kenny, M. (eds), *The Idea of Global Civil Society: Politics and Ethics in a Globalizing Era* (Routledge, UK) noting that the decline in local and national political participation does not necessarily mean that political thought can transfer beyond nationally grounded ideals, especially when accounting for hegemonic states like the United States.

15 Chandhoke (2002). *See also* Nowrot, K. (1999), 'Legal Consequences of Globalization: The Status of Non-Governmental Organizations Under International Law', 6 *Global Legal Studies J.* 579 noting the role of non-governmental organizations with the slavery movement, development of the Red Cross, and within the League of Nations. Their role was limited during the Cold War period however.

16 *See* e.g. Reinisch, A. and Irgel, C. (2001), 'The participation of non-governmental organizations (NGOs) in the WTO dispute settlement system', 1 *Non-State Actors and Intl. L.* 127.

17 Cullen, H. and Morrow, K. (2001), 'International civil society in international law: The growth of NGO participation', 1 *Non-State Actors and Intl. L.* 7.

actively involved in both the decision making process of international law (especially codification initiatives) along with the enforcement aspects.[18]

Non-governmental organizations' emotional and frank form of engaging international discourse moves the context outside of the state[19] given the emergence of civil society as an important linchpin in the international process and recognizing the influence that non-governmental organizations have on the state as well as within international bodies.[20] Non-governmental organizations go beyond the role of the state in given situations by enhancing the capacity of international organizations (and states) due to international networking and local understanding, enhanced relationship with the local population, willingness to take on difficult projects, and greater flexibility (such as capacity to address transnational issues).[21] Non-governmental organizations then serve to create and constitute state identities and interests in an active sense[22] by incorporating a wider variety of viewpoints and allowing for the expression by a broader representative capacity of groups.

Contending Issues and Problems

There are a number of inherent problems with non-governmental organizations that tend to call into question their viability as international actors and their effectiveness in serving as the so-called defenders of public interests.

One form of identified problem with non-governmental organizations relates to their normative legitimacy. Whose interests do non-governmental organizations actually represent, especially when considering that an

---

18 Nowrot (1999), noting the need for some form of legal regulatory framework for non-governmental organizations as a means of enhancing their legitimacy.

19 Warkentin, C. and Mingst, K. (2000), 'International Institutions, the State, and Global Civil Society in the Age of the World Wide Web', 6 *Global Governance* 237–257.

20 Lodgaard, S. (2000), 'Human Security: Concept and Operationalization', available at: http://www.hsph.%20harvard.edu/hpcr/events/hsworkshop/lodgaard.pdf.

21 Michael, S. (2002), 'The Role of NGOs in Human Security', Hauser Center for Nonprofit Organizations Working Paper No. 12 available at: http://ssrn.com/abstractid=351240, noting as well the downside to non-governmental organizations such as state antagonism and donor aid controlling the non-governmental organizations agenda.

22 Chandler, D. (2005), Constituting global civil society in Baker, G. and Chandler, D. *Global Civil Society: Contested futures* (Routledge, UK).

organisation might have been created for a particular issue relevant to a focused public interest group? Reference to the public at large clearly is a rather broad notion of interest advocacy when considering some of the more nuanced organizations that are operating within global civil society and the potential for inconsistent opinions within local groups or minority factions. Certain organizations maintain goals that might inherently conflict with the political or religious structure of the state, or rely upon extreme views that challenge the very essence of the state's existence.[23] How is one to distinguish between legitimate or illegitimate views when addressing organizations calling for extreme social change or claiming irregularities in the political process? There also is an inherent lack of fairness of process and minimal internal oversight for non-governmental organizations, a rather surprising result for bodies that supposedly are calling upon state actors to behave in a more democratic fashion.

Further, there is no clear indication that a special interest has been created between the organisation and the individuals or groups that they seek to represent. There certainly is no level of accountability to groups, especially in instances where cultural policies might clash or create internal tensions within a group. This is especially a problem for grassroots based organizations, where the clash between cultural values is quite stark, with many groups desiring different end results than the one's being espoused by non-governmental organizations.

Another difficulty relates to the manner by which non-governmental organizations participate in the system. Referred to as voice accountability, the problem essentially relates to what a non-governmental organisation might claim on behalf of a particular interest group and the basis of their authority for making such a claim.[24] Many times, an organisation is heavily influenced by Western-oriented values, especially when adopting a global oriented stance or when operating under a specific monetary grant, at the expense of the local population's values or cultural perceptions of a problem.[25] Indeed, many organizations will make the claim of legitimacy

---

23 *See* e.g. Salih, M. (2002), *Islamic NGOs in Africa: The Promise and Peril of Islamic Voluntarism* (Centre of African Studies, University of Copenhagen); Blitt, R. (2004), 'Who Will Watch the Watchdogs? Human Rights, Non Governmental Organizations and the Case for Regulation', 10 *Buff. H. Rts. L. Rev.* 261.

24 Slimm, H. (2002), 'By What Authority? The Legitimacy and Accountability of Non-Governmental Organizations', *Journal of Humanitarian Assistance*, available at: www.jha.ac/articles/a082htm.

25 While Slimm (2002), calls for greater accountability and legitimacy, he does note that too much control can lead to greater bureaucracy and a lessening of

based upon their connection to an international human rights cause without necessarily considering the views and perceptions of the local population and its cultural construct. This of course begs questions regarding who establishes the agenda to create focus issues and on the basis of what values? This is especially a problem for a cosmopolitan account of international relations whereby the global polity from above operates to create and instil changes and influence the state.[26]

Another related problem is that both the internal and external processes of global civil society are linked to the power structure of the state and its political interests as a means for imposing change. Global civil society actors are prone towards pre-defined notions of sovereignty, being compelled to rely on the state as a central influencing factor for creating change as well as the engagement capacity of the international system. Such reliance however discounts the important role of local actors who have a clearer perception of the issues needing attention. This is often compounded by an agenda that is linked with Westernised perceptions of problems and solutions, especially when factoring in the source of funding for many of the civil society actors that tends to heavily influence the focus of activity.

Indeed, non-governmental organizations oftentimes are part of the state/market construct, using the market process to benefit their specific cause,[27] thereby reflecting a strong Northern/Eurocentric focus at the expense of the relative values of a local population.[28] Furthermore, non-governmental organizations become entrenched in a state-oriented process since they rely on states to pressure other state actors (assuming the targeted state is even prone to such pressures). In a constructivist context for example this can be problematic because one is relying on the more powerful states to engage change.[29] A state-oriented process also makes it difficult to

---

effectiveness should the process become overly professional.

26 Baker, G. (2005), 'Saying global civil society with rights', 114 in Baker, G. and Chandler, D. (eds), *Global Civil Society: Contested Futures* (Routledge, UK).

27 Chandhoke (2002).

28 Gamble and Kenny (2005) at 31; Baker (2005) at 120; Lehr-Lehnardt, R. (2005) 'Non-Governmental Organization Legitimacy: Reassessing Democracy, Accountability, and Transparency', *Cornell Law School LLM Paper Series*, Paper #6, available at: http://lsr.nellco.org/cornell/lps/clacp/6. The author notes that too strong a focus on democracy could limit the strive for progressive development and narrow the interests of such organizations.

29 Chandler (2005) at 107 noting that 'moral change depends on the powerful, rather than the struggle of the powerless.'

properly quantify the actual effects and success rate given the variety of influences and interests that are operating at the same time.[30] The result is a system that merely shifted the strategies and tactics of the state to another venue, while providing an additional platform from which to protect and maintain the key interests of a state.

There also is the problem of internal differences between the different organizations. Non-governmental organizations might be striving for a similar cause, but it does not mean that they all represent a similar method or even agree on the desired outcome. There is inherent indecision and at times a rather damaging splintering of issues that tends to eviscerate the developing form of social relationships.[31] Non-governmental organizations maintain specific mandates and focus issues, such that even with a degree of accountability in the process, the struggle becomes an ends-oriented process, with the goal of asserting the moral claims of those not properly represented in the state political process.[32] While maintaining shared beliefs, the variety of approaches influence social and political action in different ways, indicating that the point of focus need not be on the actions of the state, but rather the relationships that exist within and among the various existing social networks.[33]

Reconsidering the Framework

Global civil society and non-governmental organizations incorporate a broad range of influences that span the economic sphere given links to influential donors and the focus on markets, broader "ideals" like human rights naturally associated (albeit sometimes incorrectly) with non-governmental organizations, political influences both external to non-governmental organizations as well as emanating from within such organizations, and matters relating to the overall state-social relationship.[34] The variety of interest at work in the global civil society context implies a rather complex form of process that is subject to a barrage of persuasion

---

30 Chandler (2005), at 160–162.

31 Lord, J. (2004), 'Mirror Mirror on the Wall: Voice Accountability and Non-Governmental Organizations in Human Rights Standard Setting', 5 *Seton Hall J. Diplomacy and Intl. Rel.* 93 (referring specifically to the Peoples with Disabilities Convention, where non-governmental organizations displayed a host of differing opinions and approaches towards the manner and form of protection to be accorded).

32 Chandler (2005) at 184.

33 Lord (2004) refers to this as network accountability.

34 *See* e.g. Stiles (2000) at 44.

and opinions from a host of different actors. It is this aspect of non-governmental organizations however that affords the opportunity to adopt a broader form view of the process, whereby the constant resistance exhibited by non-governmental organizations coupled with the broad array of viewpoints[35] provide the grounds for moving the framework of study into an alternate context of examination.

The essence of examining global civil society and non-governmental organizations is to provide a platform from which to consider how social movements external to the state can play an active role in developing policy and shaping society. The centre of power as emanating from the state has been shifted to apparatus both above and below the state. Global civil society is influential in the domestic and international sphere, including within international organizations,[36] in a manner that has tended to alter the international order. Global civil society allows for consideration of the state and its functioning role from a point of resistance outside a state-centric framework that incorporates a multiplicity of actors. The assessment moves towards a relational framework, examining the manner by which political choices are made and considering how the relationship between the various actors develops given their mission to shape and influence policies and mandates. An important result then is to acknowledge the position of non-governmental organizations and allow them to pursue their goals, without an imposition of a pre-defined concept regarding global ethics or pre-imposed limits to the international arena formerly the exclusive domain of the state. The various influences deriving from non-governmental organizations reflect emerging roots of some form of international governance that recognises the derivation of power from a host of non-state actors. Rather than examining non-governmental organizations pursuant to their link to the state and its attendant institutions that tends to limit their scope and operation, it would be of greater benefit to consider the altered power arrangements that have resulted from the ongoing resistance offered by non-governmental organizations that have shifted the capacity to govern outside the realm of the state.[37]

35 Including those associated with the state due to financial ties or as a result of a mandated agenda such as the link to human rights, as well more extreme non-governmental organizations that espouse radical views.

36 Park, S. (2004), 'The Role of Transnational Advocacy Networks in Reconstituting International Organisation Identities', 5 *Seton Hall J. Diplomacy and Intl. Rel.* 79.

37 Rajagopal, B. (2003), *International Law from Below: Development, Social Movements and Third World Resistance* (Cambridge University Press, UK) at Chapter 7.

What transpires then is not a clearly defined sphere for global civil society or a normative framework for determining the legitimacy of the participating actors, a problematic proposition given the subjective orientations of the state towards specific viewpoints or desired movements, but actually an ongoing form of discourse between the various actors therein. The variety of global civil society actors are beginning to assert their views as a counterbalance to the state, going beyond the reliance on human rights or state mandated viewpoints as grounds for legitimising their stance to incorporate all perceptions and assertions. The international framework is expanding to allow for the operative incorporation of non-governmental organizations into international discourse, in a manner that embraces the at times natural resistance of non-governmental organizations to state directives and initiatives.

Global civil society then is not solely a movement of resistance emanating from below (although grassroots movement and local perceptions are an important part of the process), but actually a reflection of ongoing power relations between the variety of actors, all of whom maintain some form of role and influence within the discourse, as well as being subject to the influential drives of the other participating actors (including the state). Thus, global civil society is not an ideal form of democracy whereby all have the opportunity for expression. Reference to democratic ideals would tend to limit the development of non-governmental organizations and stifle the discourse pursuant to pre-conceived political notions, as reflected in the problems noted *supra*. Rather, global civil society and non-governmental organizations are a reflection of emerging forms of governmentality that incorporate a variety of perceptions and approaches all of whom wield power to play an active role in the international framework.[38]

Non-governmental organizations demonstrate that the state as such does not maintain the capacity for power over and above the variety of existing non-state actors, but actually a host of perceptions and approaches are incorporated into the network of power due to their potential for engaging and influencing domestic and international actors within the ongoing discourse. The actions and potential for influence exhibited by non-governmental organizations demonstrate the complex role of power that is at work, going beyond the capacity of the state. The activity of non-governmental organizations involves discourse formations that go towards the creation of power (and not merely responding to state's power through

---

38 Amoore, L. and Langley, P. (2005), 'Global civil society and global governmentality', in Germain, R. and Kenny, M. (eds), *The Idea of Global Civil Society: Politics and Ethics in a Globalizing Era* (Routledge, UK) at 147–148.

its influence or initiatives) since non-governmental organizations perform an independent role at the local, national, and international level.[39] Of course, power operates in a multifaceted fashion that does not discount the role of the state, however non-governmental organizations also play a significant role in this development.

The noted problems concerning internal disputes and divisions within non-governmental organizations actually demonstrate their capacity for operation. Global civil society is not a cohesive unit of actors with a clear agenda or mandate, unlike the more formalised sovereign state that traditionally has been associated with specific interests and goals as grounds for action. Rather, similar to the current international framework, global civil society entails the incorporation of a host of issue-oriented actors into the discourse, presenting conflicting and even radical views. This capacity for inclusion makes it difficult for the international system to conceive given the open-ended framework.

Non-governmental organizations provide constant alterations of viewpoints and issues that forces further development of the international process. The importance of their role lies not solely in the ability to alter the norms or regulations that exist, but actually play a part in the constitutive aspects of the international process regarding the manner by which such norms or regulations are formed.[40] This is an important step when accounting for greater privatisation and the diminishing role of the state since many potential targets for change will begin to assume, and even dominate, the constitutive role formerly inhabited by the state, thereby removing issues from the public arena.[41]

The use of power as a productive tool however affords the opportunity to reconstitute the international process that recognises an active role for non-governmental organizations, as being part of the discourse and part of the reality in which international law operates. Examining the operative capacities of non-governmental organizations then is not linked to the state or to engaging in empirical studies regarding success; rather power plays

39 Amoore and Langley (2005) at 151.

40 Lipschutz, R. (2005), 'Global civil society and global governmentality: Resistance, reform or resignation?', in Baker, G. and Chandler, D. (eds) *Global Civil Society: Contested Futures* (Routledge, UK) at 178.

41 Lipschutz (2005) at 179, noting this problem with corporate regulation, since even with the move towards oversight of corporations for human rights violations, the manner of regulatory control remains in the hands of the private actors.

a productive role whereby the various assertions of non-governmental organizations generate new webs of power that address the constitutive aspects of international law as well. The transformative approach to power shifts attention from the state as the central player to one whereby all actors maintain some form of influence. Non-governmental organizations participate in the issues and agenda setting as a means of asserting their power potential in international issues, allowing for discourse to continue not as a means of achieving the truth or final understanding, but as an ongoing notion of resistance that tends to highlight the limits in which we operate.

Conclusion

Given the goal of proposing an alternative approach to international law, it is important to account for the various actors that have emerged as actual role players in establishing agenda issues and shaping international norms. The advent of global civil society clearly involves non-state actors like non-governmental organizations as imperative participants that merit consideration of where and how they conform to the international framework.

Granted there are a number of key problems with non-governmental organizations given their potential for being overly prone to external influences along with internal divisions and pre-defined mandates. Greater professionalism or regulation however will not necessarily lead to greater efficacy, but actually is rooted in notions of sovereign authority that will tend to eviscerate the very effectiveness of non-governmental organizations that is being sought.

One avenue for addressing these issues, as well as according non-governmental organizations their proper role, is via a transformative approach that moves the power framework to a productive context. In that sense, the variety of global civil society actors can effectively participate in the international process without being subject to externally determined values that incorrectly rely on subjective perceptions and interpretations as grounds for questioning their legitimacy and active role. Rather, non-governmental organizations can participate in the constitutive process to engage the underlying sources of problems and divisions in the international framework.

Chapter 8

Conclusion

Professor Kennedy recently noted that given the current situation of international political culture, we need to worry less about

> …making the legal culture more dense. Rather [that] we should worry about finding sites and opportunities for increasing the possibility for politics, for contestation of the outcomes and procedures of the existing legal regime. The difficulty is how to do that.[1]

The proposals and ideas mentioned in this book are an attempt to begin this journey of contestation, of considering a context that embraces gaps and conflicts. The international system has become a rather complex and diffuse network of activity and relations involving a host of influences from a variety of actors. The capacity to raise one's voice and influence policy is very real, such as to suggest that Foucault's understanding of power and knowledge is a proper starting point for at least providing a context by which to comprehend the international system.[2] In essence, Foucault provides analytic devices and various interpretations as the means for considering alternative approaches that will not necessarily provide answers as such, but rather embrace the struggle and resistance inherent within the international system.

What has been developed thus far in this book is a starting point from which to consider additional areas and issues within the international context. The goal is to offer a framework by which one can refer to Foucault to better explicate international law. Each chapter focused on different aspects of international law, accounting for state-state relations via recognition, notions of the sources of international law and its development via custom, human rights and relations between the state and other actors via the freedom of religion or belief, and the emergence of alternative

---

1 Kennedy, D. (2003), 'Contestation of the Outcomes and Procedures of the Existing Legal Regime', 16 *Leiden J. Intl. L.* 915–917 at 915.

2 Hindess, B. (2005), 'Politics as Government: Michel Foucault's Analysis of Political Reason', 30 *Alternatives* 389 notes that the undefined nature of the international system's centre implies a broader form of ongoing relationships between a wide variety of actors beyond the state.

paradigms via consideration of non-governmental organisations and global civil society, as well as human security. The basic overlying theme was to consider these issues from a Foucauldian perspective that elucidated the manner of relations between the participating actors from a transformative context, accounting for, in particular, the importance of discourse and the ensuing role of power and knowledge in an operative fashion.

Looking more specifically to the issues addressed in this book, a host of issues can be further examined and explicated. The chapter on recognition of states for example can be expanded by considering concepts like emerging factions within states such as autonomous regions or the claims of ethnic groups who are asserting their position within the international system. A process-oriented approach will provide for their amelioration and consideration at an important juncture in time where internal conflicts and ethnic tensions are rapidly rising within states that previously adhered to a rather static and pre-defined notion of the social construct. Adopting a transgressive approach would tend towards greater allowances in a manner that could lessen social tension and conflict.

Another example is the chapter on customary international law. Further discussion is merited on its relation with other international law sources, principally treaties, which also could be well served by a discourse orientation. Specific examples of the historical progression of custom would also be assisted by reference to Foucault and his genealogical approach to social development. This can allow for the incorporation of political views and social perceptions as they have developed within a historical narrative while more readily allowing for subjective approaches that can serve to better elucidate the emergence of custom.

Chapter 5, regarding international human rights and the right to freedom of religion or belief, can be even further developed by considering seminal problems within the international human rights system, such as relativism and non-Western approaches to rights, as well as considering the incorporating of a communitarian approach to human rights. A Foucauldian perspective can allow, at the very least, for a reflection of these approaches and assist to improve upon the existing human rights system. Similarly, human security is an emerging concept that merits further consideration given that it opens up international law to new vistas. While different contexts by which to apply human security warrant examination, referring to Foucault can develop and entrench human security by recognising the need for constant change and evaluation that tends to stress the outer limits, rather than seek a normative solution.

Further study and examination that can assist with moving forward the development of international law is merited. Notably, Foucault's understanding of power and how it conforms to the current international system is important. It certainly opens the door for non-state actors other than non-governmental organisations that exist in alternative frameworks external to the state, such as the position of indigenous peoples within the international framework. Indeed, considering minority factions or indigenous peoples highlights as well some of the problems noted with Foucault's approach concerning partisan politics within the state[3] as well as his assumption concerning the inherent discontinuity of discourse.[4] Foucault allows for the beginning of a shift in the social goal such that it need not be considered from the perspective of the overall majority will, nor as succumbing to the tyranny of the minority. Rather, the various factions serve to elucidate the different perceptions and opinions that exist within the state, engaging in ongoing social discourse that would acknowledge a role and position for the multitude of factions emerging in societies around the world. Indigenous peoples in particular would maintain a broader social platform to participate and assert their interests in a manner that recognises their social position and rights. Indeed, the underlying difficulties faced by the drafters of the recent Declaration on the Rights of Indigenous Peoples adopted by the United Nations Human Rights Council in June, 2006, centred on the struggle between sovereign control by the state versus according degrees of autonomy and self determination to indigenous peoples. The struggle however can be placed in a broader plane outside the state-sovereign context that cannot always account for territorial rights of other entities. Rather, the power struggle over self determination or autonomous control is part of the ongoing social discourse that is being engaged by non-state entities who maintain an entrenched social position with capacity to influence and create change.

A similar context can be applied to other troubling aspects of international law and minority factions, particularly the plight of migrant workers. It has proven quite difficult to create some form of rights protection for migrant workers yet they are mercilessly exposed to excessive rights violations. Moving away from a normative centred

---

3 *See* e.g. Hindess (2005), noting the need for considering specific interests raised by minority groups who deviate from the overall common good as defined by social forces within the state.

4 Galindo, G. (2005), 'Marti Koskenniemi and the Historiographical Turn in International Law', 16 *E. J. Intl. L.* 539 notes that just as Foucault made inherent assumptions about discontinuities, so too does Koskenniemi assume a discontinuity in international law towards the end of the nineteenth century.

notion towards one of power and knowledge opens the door for their consideration and recognition to attain social status given their role in local discourse and capacity to engage in social change.

Another important example that has risen to the fore in the international system is the role of corporations as influencing developments and policy. With the advent of globalisation and the heightened role of commercial players as influencing policy decisions, along with the greater reliance by states on private entities to provide public goods, it is important to consider the manner by which corporations and other private organisations conform to the system. Certainly within the human rights context, the role of corporations has been recognised, to the extent that they have acquired a form of international responsibility and accountability. Yet, to brand these developments as reflecting emerging international law would be troubling for those rooted in a state-centred system. A Foucauldian approach however opens the door for acknowledging the role of corporations as international actors, thereby presenting the means for properly considering their active role within the international system.

In a broader sense, Foucault also can assist in other areas of international law. For example, consideration of judicial-like bodies external to the state that maintain operative facilities, such as the International Criminal Court, could be assisted in enhancing their functional capacities. As these entities develop, it is important to consider them within an effective framework of examination that recognises their role and standing vis-à-vis other actors (especially the state), thereby allowing for their entrenchment within the international system. Similarly, examining the manner by which various international organs operate, especially as politics and law become further enmeshed even in so-called neutral bodies like the United Nation's International Court of Justice, can be better served via the approaches of Foucault.

Disciplines are beginning to naturally combine, especially when considering the growth in capacity for engaging in communication and rapid acquisition of information. The changes that have derived from these abilities are apparent to all international actors, with a search for alternative frameworks to address these changes. Yet, too often international discourse is confined to liberalist traditions and reference to democratic systems as the sole legitimate form of states, international organisations and non-state actors. State interests and political rhetoric tends to hide behind these so-called altruist movements without considering the realities of the claims being made or the manner by which the liberal tradition and its orientation towards capitalist markets entrenches Western-oriented methodologies. Alternative approaches to power are necessary to uproot this tendency, not to eviscerate the international system but to prevent malaise and disillusionment by the various international and state actors that could lead to a breakdown of the system. It is important to provide notions that allow for a broader spectrum of views and ideas without summarily dismissing perceptions that are inherently contrary to what is understood to be the legitimate system that is in essence linked to subjective interpretations. Reference to the Foucauldian approach can assist with moving international discourse forward, thereby allowing for some form of design by which one can grasp the system and progress to new avenues and heights. While such a task might not be all that easy for an international system that is in essence seeking some form of legal certainty, a natural inclination for the legally trained, it is worth noting the following words of Foucault:

> instead of providing a basis for what already exists, instead of going over with bold strokes lines that have already been sketched, instead of finding reassurance in this return and final confirmation, instead of completing the blessed circle that announces, after innumerable stratagems and as many nights, that all is saved, one is forced to advance beyond familiar territory, far from the certainties to which one is accustomed, towards an as yet uncharted land and unforeseeable conclusion.[5]

5 Foucault, M. (1969, trans. 1972), *The Archaeology of Knowledge* (Routledge, UK) at Chapter 2.

Bibliography

International Documents

Treaties

Universal Declaration of Human Rights
International Covenant on Civil and Political Rights
European Convention on Human Rights and Fundamental Freedoms
American Convention on Human Rights

UN Documents

GA Third Committee, Fifth Session, meeting 288 (1950)
GA, Third Committee, Sixth Session, meeting 367 (1951)
GA Third Committee, Fifth Session, meetings 306 (1950)
GA, Third Committee, Fifteenth Session, meeting 1021–1028 (1960)
GA Third Committee, Fifteenth Session, meeting 1021 (1960)
GA Third Committee, Fifteenth Session, A/4625, Agenda Item 34 (1960)

E/CN.4/SR.60 (1948)
E/CN.4/85 (1948)
E/CN.4/82/Add.8 and 12 (1948)
E/CN.4/SR.161 (1950)
E/CN.4/528 (1951)
E/CN.4/SR.319 (1952)
E/CN.4/RES/2000/23
E/CN.4/2000/65

Human Rights Committee, General Comment Number 22 (1993)
Human Rights Committee, General Comment Number 31 (2004)

United Nations Commission on Human Security (2003), 'Human Security Now', available at: www.humansecurity-chs.org/finalreport/index.html

Judicial Decisions

International

ICJ Advisory Opinion Legal Consequences of the Construction of a Wall in the Occupied Palestinian Territory decided 9/7/04, available at: http://www.icj-cij.org/icjwww/idocket/imwp/imwpframe.htm

Regional

16616/90 *Vereniging v. Netherlands* 46 D&R 200 (1986)
14307/88 *Kokkinakis v. Greece* 17 EHRR 397 (1993)
16278/90 *Karaduman v. Turkey* 74 D&R 93 (1993)
7805/77 *Church of Scientology v. Sweden* 16 D&R 68 (1979)
27417/95 *Cha'are Shalom Ve Tsedek v. France* Decision of 27/6/00
74/1995/580/666 *Valsamis v. Greece* 1996-VI Rep. Judg. & Dec. 2312
44774/98 *Leyla Sahin v. Turkey* decided 10/11/05, available at: http://cmiskp.echr.coe.int/tkp197/viewhbkm.asp?action=open&table=1132746FF1FE2A468ACCBCD1763D4D8149&key=17671&sessionId=5856548&skin=hudoc-en&attachment=true

Domestic

Mingtai v. UPS Case Number 9815088, Ninth Circuit, 5/25/99, available at: http://caselaw.lp.findlaw.com/cgi-bin/getcase.pl?court=9th&navby=case&no=9815088
Taiwan v. Dist Ct Case Number No. 9770375, Ninth Circuit, 10/16/97, available at: http://caselaw.lp.findlaw.com/cgi-bin/getcase.pl?court=9th&navby=case&no=9770375
Jacques v. Hilton 569 F.Supp. 729 (N.J.Dist.Ct. 1983)

Books

Alkire, S. (2003) 'Concepts of Human Security', in Chen, L., Fukuda-Parr, S. and Seidensticker, S. (eds), *Human Insecurity in a Globalised World* (Harvard University Press, USA).

Allen, B. (1998), 'Foucault and Modern Political Philosophy', 164–198 in Moss, J. (ed.) *The Later Foucault: Politics and Philosophy* (Sage Pub., London).

Amoore, L. and Langley, P. (2005), 'Global civil society and global governmentality', in Germain, R. and Kenny, M. (eds),*The Idea of Global Civil Society: Politics and Ethics in a Globalizing Era* (Routledge, UK).

Axworthy, L. (2004), 'Human Security: An Opening for UN Reform', 245–260 in Price, R. and Zacher, M. (eds), *The United Nations and Global Security* (Palgrave, Macmillan, NY).

Baker, G. (2005), 'Saying global civil society with rights', 114 in Baker, G. and Chandler, D. (eds), *Global Civil Society: Contested Futures* (Routledge, UK).

Baker, G. and Chandler, D. (2005), 'Introduction: global civil society and the future of world politics', in Baker, G. and Chandler, D. (eds), *Global Civil Society: Contested Futures* (Routledge, UK).

Barker, P. (2000), *Michel Foucault: An Introduction* (Edinburgh University Press, UK).

Bernauer, J. and Mahon, M. (1994), 'The Ethics of Michel Foucault', 153 in Gutting, G. (ed.), *The Cambridge Companion to Foucault* (Cambridge University Press, USA).

Biersteker, T. and Weber, C. (1996), 'The Social Construction of State Sovereignty', 1 in Biersteker, T. and Weber, C. (eds.) *State Sovereignty as Social Construct* (Cambridge University Press, UK).

Byers, M. (1999), *Custom, Power and the Power of Rules* (Oxford University Press, UK).

Chandhoke, N. (2002), 'Limits of Global Civil Society', in Glasius, M., Kaldor, M. and Anheier, H. (eds), *Global Civil Society* (Centre for the Study of Global Civil Society, UK), available at: http://www lse.ac.uk/Depts/global/yearbook02chapters.htm.

Chandler, D. (2005), *Constructing Global Civil Society: Morality and Power in International Relations* (Palgrave Macmillan, UK).

Chandler, D. (2005), 'Constituting global civil society', in Baker, G. and Chandler, D. *Global Civil Society: Contested Futures* (Routledge, UK).

Cheng, B. (1983), 'Custom: The Future of General State Practice in a Divided World', 513 in Macdonald, R. and Johnston, D. (eds), *The Structure and Process of International Law: Essays in Legal Philosophy, Doctrine and Theory* (M. Nijhoff, Netherlands).

Chigara, B. (2001), *Legitimacy Deficit in Custom: A Deconstructionist Critique* (Ashgate, UK).

Connelly, W. (1999), *Why I am not a Secularist* (University of Minnesota Press, USA).

Crawford, J. (1979), *The Creation of States in International Law* (Clarendon Press, UK).

D'Amato, A. (1971), *The Concept of Custom in International Law* (Cornell University Press, NY).

de Lupis, I. (1987), *The Concept of International Law* (Nordstedts Forlag, Stockholm).

Evans, C. (2000), *Article 9 and the European Convention of Human Rights* (Oxford University Press, UK).

Evans, M. (1997), *Religious Liberty and International Law in Europe* (Cambridge University Press, UK).

Forsythe, D. (2000), *Human Rights in International Relations* (Cambridge University Press, UK).

Foucault, M. (1969, trans. 1972), *The Archaeology of Knowledge* (Routledge, UK).

Foucault, M. (1977), *Discipline and Punish: The Birth of the Prison* (Pantheon Books, NY).

Foucault, M. (1980) *Power/Knowledge: Selected Interviews and Other Writings 1972–1977* (Harvester Press, Sussex).

Foucault, M. (1989) *Foucault Live (Interviews, 1966–84)* Lotringer, S. (ed.) (Semiotext(e), NY).

Foucault, M. (1997), 'Society Must Be Defended', in Rabinow, P. (ed.) *Michel Foucault, Ethic: Essential works of Foucault_1954–1984, Volume 1* (The New Press, USA).

Frank, T. (1990) *The Power of Legitimacy Among Nations* (Oxford University Press, UK).

Fuchs, J. (1987), 'The Phenomenon of Conscience: Subject-Orientation and Object-Orientation', 27–47 in Zecha, G. and Weingartner, P. (eds) *Conscience: An Interdisciplinary View* (Reidel Publishing Co., Holland).

Gamble, A. and Kenny. M. (2005), 'Ideological contestation, transnational civil society, and global politics', in Germain, R. and Kenny, M. (eds), *The Idea of Global Civil Society: Politics and Ethics in a Globalizing Era* (Routledge, UK).

Goldsmith, J. and Posner, E. (2005) *The Limits of International Law* (Oxford University Press, NY).

Gordon, C. (1991), 'Governmental Rationality: An Introduction', 1–53 in Burchell, G., Gordon, C. and Miller, P. (eds), *The Foucault Effect: Studies in Governmentality* (University of Chicago Press, USA).

Hammer, L. (2001), *The International Human Right to Freedom of Conscience: Some Suggestions for its Development and Application* (Ashgate, UK).

Hunt, A. and Wickham G (1994), *Foucault and Law: Towards a Sociology of Law as Governance* (Pluto Press, London)

International Law Association (2000), Final Report of the Committee on Formation of Customary (General) International Law, available at: http://www.ila-hq.org/html/layout_committee.htm.

Ivison, D. (1998), 'The Disciplinary Moment: Foucault, Law, and the Reinscription of Rights', in Mass, J. (ed.), *The Later Foucault* (Sage Publications, UK).

Jones, R. (1999), *Security Strategy and Critical Theory* (L. Rienner Pub., USA).

Kenny, M. and Germain, R. (2005), 'The idea(l) of global civil society', in Germain, R. and Kenny, M. (eds), *The Idea of Global Civil Society: Politics and ethics in a Globalizing Era* (Routledge, UK).

Koskenniemi, M. (1989), *From Apology to Utopia: The Structure of International Legal Argument* (Finnish Lawyers Pub. Comp., Helsinki).

Krasner, S. (1999), *Sovereignty: Organized Hypocrisy* (Princeton University Press, NJ),

Lipschutz, R. (2005), 'Global civil society and global governmentality: Resistance, reform or resignation?', 171 in Baker, G. and Chandler, D. (eds), *Global Civil Society: Contested Futures* (Routledge, UK).

Lukes, S. (2005), *Power: A Radical View* (Palgrave Macmillan, NY, 2nd ed.)

Malpas, J. (2001), 'Governing Theory: Ontology, Methodology and the Critique of Metaphysics', 125–140 in Wickham, G. and Pavlich, G. (eds), *Rethinking Law, Society and Governance: Foucault's Bequest* (Hart Pub., Oxford).

McCarthy, T. (1998), 'The Critique of Impure Reason: Foucault and the Frankfurt School', in Kelly, M. (ed.) *Critique and Power: Recasting the Foucault/Habermas Debate* (MIT Press, USA).

McHoul, A. and Grace, W. (1997), *A Foucault Primer: Discourse, Power and the Subject* (New York University Press, USA),

Meron, T. (1989), *Human Rights and Humanitarian Norms as Customary Law* (Oxford University Press, UK),

Moskos, C. and Chambers, J. (eds) (1993), *The New Conscientious Objection: From Sacred to Secular Resistance* (Oxford University Press, NY),

Parekh, B. (2000), *Rethinking Multiculturalism: Cultural Diversity and Political Theory* (Macmillan Press, London),

Rajagopal, B. (2003), *International Law from Below: Development, Social Movements and Third World Resistance* (Cambridge University Press, UK).

Reinicke, W. and Witte, J. (2000), 'Interdependence, Globalization, and Sovereignty: The Role of Non-binding International Legal Accords'. 75–100 in Shelton, D. (ed.) *Commitment and Compliance: The Role of Non-Binding Norms in the International Legal System* (Oxford University Press, UK).

Reisman, W. M. and Suzuki, E. (1976), 'Recognition and Social Change in International Law: A Prologue for Decisionmaking', 403–470 in Reisman, W. M. and Weston, B. (eds), *Toward World Order and Human Dignity: Essays in Honor of Myres S. McDougal* (Macmillan, NY).

Robinson, D. and Oosterveld, V. (2001), 'The Evolution of International Humanitarian Law', 161–170 in McRae, R. and Hubert, D. (eds), *Human Security and the New Diplomacy: Protecting People, Promoting Peace* (McGill-Queens University Press, Montreal).

Rouse J. (1994), 'Power/Knowledge', 111 in Gutting, G. (ed.) *The Cambridge Companion to Foucault* (Cambridge University Press, USA).

Salih, M. (2002), *Islamic NGOs in Africa: The Promise and Peril of Islamic Voluntarism* (Centre of African Studies, University of Copenhagen).

Schachter, O. (1989) 'Entangled Treaty and Custom' 717 in Dinstein, Y. and Tabory, M. (eds) *International Law at a Time of Perplexity* (M. Nijhoff, Netherlands).

Scholte, J. (1999), 'Security and Community in a Globalizing World', 59–84 in Thomas, C. and Wilkin P. (eds), *Globalisation, Human Security and the African Experience* (L. Rienner Pub., USA).

Scholte, J. (2000), *Globalization: A Critical Introduction* (Palgrave, UK).

Simons, J. (1995) *Foucault and the Political* (Routledge, UK).

Stiles, K. (2000), 'Grassroots Empowerment: States, non-state actors and global policy formulation', in Higgott, R., Underhill, G. and Bieler, A. (eds), *Non-State Actors and Authority in the Global System* (Routledge, UK).

Strong, D. (1996), 'Contested Sovereignty: the social construction of colonial imperialism', 22 in Biersteker, T. and Weber, C. (eds), *State Sovereignty as Social Construct* (Cambridge University Press, UK).

Tahzib, B. (1996), *Freedom of Religion or Belief: Ensuring Effective International Protection* (Nijhoff, The Netherlands).

Talmon, S. (1997), 'The Legal Consequence of (non) Recognition: Cyprus and the Council of Europe', 57 in Evans, M. (ed.) *Aspects of Statehood and Institutionalism in Contemporary Europe* (Dartmouth, UK).

Talmon, S. (1998), *Recognition of Governments in International Law With Particular Reference to Governments in Exile* (Oxford University Press, UK).

Taylor, C. (1989), *Sources of the Self; The Making of the Modern Identity* (Cambridge University Press, UK).

Thomas, C. (1999), 'Introduction', 1 in Thomas, C. and Wilkin P. (eds), *Globalisation, Human Security and the African Experience* (L. Rienner Pub., USA).

Thomas, W. (2001), *The Ethics of Destruction:Norms and Force in International Relations* (Cornell University Press, NY).

van Bijsterved, S. (2000), 'Religion, International Law and Policy in the Wider European Arena: New Dimensions and Developments', 165 in Ahdar, R. (ed.) *Law and Religion* (Ashgate, UK).

Warbrick, C. (1997) 'Recognition of States: Recent European Practice', 9 in Evans, M. (ed.) *Aspects of Statehood and Institutionalism in Contemporary Europe* (Dartmouth, UK).

Wickham, G. (2002) Foucault and Law 248–266 in Banakar, R. and Travers, M. (eds), *An Introduction to Law and Social Theory* (Hart Pub., Oxford).

Wilkin. P. (1999) 'Human Security and Class in a Global Economy', 23–33 in Thomas, C. and Wilkin P. (eds) *Globalisation, Human Security and the African Experience* (L. Rienner Pub., USA).

Witte, J. and Van der Vyver, J. (eds) (1996), *Religious Human Rights in Global Perspective* (M. Nijhoff, The Netherlands).

Articles

Acharya, A. (2001), 'Human Security: East Versus West', 56 *International Journal* 442–460.

Akehurst, M. (1974), 'Custom as a Source of International Law 1974–75', *Brit. Ybk. Intl. L.* 1.

Allot, P. (1992), 'Reconstituting Humanity – New International Law', 3 *E. J Intl. L.* 219–252.

Anderson, K. (2000), 'The Ottawa Convention Banning Landmines, the Role of International Non-governmental Organizations and the Idea of International Civil Society', 11 *E. J. Intl. L.* 91–120.

Ball, D (2004), 'Toss the Travaux? Application of the Fourth Geneva Convention to the Middle East Conflict – A Modern (Re)Assessment', 79 *N. Y. U. L. Rev.* 990.

Bassiouni, C. (1990), 'A Functional Approach to "General Principles of International Law"', 11 *Mich. J. Intl. L.* 7

Baxter, H. (1996), 'Bringing Foucault into Law and Law into Foucault', 48 *Stanford Law Review* 449.

Baxter, R. (1970), 'Treaties and Custom', I *Recueil des Cours* 25.

Benhabib, S. (2005), 'On the Alleged Conflict between Democracy and International Law', 19 *Ethics and Intl. Affairs* 85–101.

Berman, P. (2006), 'Seeing Beyond the Limits of International Law', 84 *Tex. L. R.* 1265.

Blitt, R. (2004), 'Who Will Watch the Watchdogs? Human Rights, Non Governmental Organizations and the Case for Regulation', 10 *Buff. H. Rts. L. Rev.* 261–398.

Bodansky, D. (1995), 'Customary (And Not So Customary) International Environmental Law', 3 *Indiana J. Global Legal Studies* 105–119.

Boyle, A. (2004), 'International law before national courts: Some problems from a common law perspective', 4 *Non-State Actors and International Law* 59–64.

Bradley, C. and Goldsmith, J. (1997), 'Customary International Law as Federal Common Law: A Critique of the Modern Position', 110 *Harv. L. Rev.* 815.

Brandt and Kaplan (1996), 'The Tension Between Women's Rights and Religious Rights: Reservations to CEDAW by Egypt, Bangladesh and Tunisia', XII *Journal of Law and Religion* 105.

Bruderlein, C. (2001), 'People's Security as a New Means of Global Stability', 83 *Intl. Rev. Red Cross* 353–366.

Byron, C. (2001), 'Armed Conflicts: International or Non-International?', 6 *J. Conflict Studies* 63.

Carty, A. (1991), 'Critical International Law: Recent Trends in the Theory of International Law', 2 *E. J. Intl. L.* 66–96.

Constable, M. (1991), 'Foucault and Walzer: Sovereignty, Strategy, and the State', 24 *Polity* 269.

Crillo-Suarez, A. (1999), 'Hors de Logique: Contemporary Issues in International Humanitarian Law as Applied to Internal Armed Conflict', 15 *Am. U Intl. Rev* 1.

Cullen, H. and Morrow, K. (2001), 'International civil society in international law: The growth of NGO participation', 1 *Non-State Actors and Intl. L.* 7–39.

de Lisle, J. (2000), 'The Chinese Puzzle of Taiwan's Status', 44 *Orbis* 35.

Danilenko, G. (1988), 'The Theory of Customary International Law', 31 *Germ. Ybk. Intl. L.* 9.

Edge, P. (1998), 'The European Court of Human Rights and Religious Rights', 46 *International and Comparative Law Quarterly* 680.

Edge, P. (1996), 'Current Problems in Article 9 of The European Convention on Human Rights', 1996 *Juridical Review* 42.

Elias, O. (1995), 'The Nature of the Subjective Element in Customary International Law', 44 *Intl. Comp. L. Q.* 501.

Epps, V. (2001), 'Book Review: "The Recognition of States: Law and Practice in Debate and Evolution", by Thomas D. Grant', 95 *A. J. I. L.* 252.

Fidler, D. (1996), 'Challenging the Concept of Custom: Perspectives on the Future of Customary International Law', 39 *Germ. Ybk. Intl. L.* 198.

Fox, G. and Nolte, G (2002), 'Intolerant Democracies', 36 *Harv. Intl. L.J.* 1.

Galindo, G. (2005), 'Marti Koskenniemi and the Historiographical Turn in International Law', 16 *E. J. Intl. L.* 539.

Garcia F. (2005), 'Globalization and the Theory of International Law', *B.C. Law School Faculty Papers*, paper #93, available at: http://lsr.nellco.org/bc/bclsfp/papers/93 .

Georgiev, D. (1993), 'Politics or Rule of Law: Deconstruction and Legitimacy in International Law', 4 *E. J. Intl. L.* 1–14.

Goldsmith, J. and Posner, E. (1999), 'A Theory of Customary International Law', 66 *U. Chi. L. Rev.* 1113.

Goodman, R. and Jenks, D. (2003), 'Towards an Institutional Theory of Sovereignty', 55 *Stan. L. Rev.* 1749.

Grayson, K. (2003), 'Securitization and the Boomerang Debate: A Rejoinder to Liotta and Smith-Windsor', 34 *Security Dialogue* 337–343.

Guzman, A. (2002), 'A Compliance-Based Theory of International Law', 90 *Calif. L. Rev.* 1823.

Hillgruber, C. (1998), 'The Admission of New States to the International Community', 9 *E. J. I. L.* 491–509.

Hindess, B. (2005), 'Politics as Government: Michel Foucault's Analysis of Political Reason', 30 *Alternatives* 389.

Hindess, B. (1997), 'Politics and Governmentality', 26 *Economy and Society* 257–272.

Hobe, S. (2002), 'The Era of Globalisation as a Challenge to International Law', 40 *Duq. L. Rev.* 655–666.

Hunt, A. (1992), 'Foucault's Expulsion of Law: Toward a Retrieval', 17 *Law and Soc. Inquiry* 1–38.

Huang, E. (2003), 'Taiwan's Status in a Changing World: United Nations Representation and Membership for Taiwan', 9 *Ann. Surv. Intl. and Comp. L.* 55.

Ivison, D. (1998), 'The Technical and the Political: Discourses of Race, Reasons of State', 7 *Social and Legal Studies* 561–566.

Kammerhofer, J. (2004), 'Uncertainty in the Formal Sources of International Law: Customary International Law and Some of its Problems', 15 *E. J. Intl. L.* 523.

Keeley, J. (1990), 'Toward a Foucauldian analysis of international regimes', 44 *Intl. Org.* 83–105.

Kelly, J. (2000), 'The Twilight of Customary International Law', 40 *Va. J. Intl. L.* 449.

Kennedy, D. (2003), 'Contestation of the Outcomes and Procedures of the Existing Legal Regime', 16 *Leiden J. Intl. L.* 915–917.

Kennedy, D. (2000), 'When Renewal Repeats: Thinking Against the Box', 32 *N. Y. U. J. Intl. L. and Pol.* 335.

Kilibarda, K. (2003), 'Selective Recognition and the Dismantling of SFR Yugoslavia; The EC's Criteria under International Law', available at: http://www.swans.com/library/art9/kkilib03.html.

Kingsbury, B. (2005), 'The International Legal Order IILJ Working Paper 2003/1', (History and Theory of International Law Series) available at: www.iilj.org.

King, G. and Murray, C. (2001), 'Rethinking Human Security', 116 *Political Science Quarterly* 585–610.

Kirgis, F. (1987), 'Custom on a Sliding Scale', 81 *Am. J. Intl. L.* 146.

Klabbers, J. (2002), 'Comment: The Curious Condition of Custom', 8 *Intl. Legal Theory* 29.

Koh, H. (1998), 'Is International Law Really State Law?' 111 *Harv. L. Rev.* 1824.

Koskenniemi, M. (1990), 'The Politics of International Law', 1 *E. J. Intl. L.* 4–32.

Krasner, S. (2003), 'The Hole in the Whole: Sovereignty, Shared Sovereignty, and International Law', 25 *Mich. J Intl. L.* 1075.

Kundmueller, M. (2002), 'The Application of Customary International Law in U.S. Courts: Custom, Convention or Pseudo-legislation?', 28 *J. Legis.* 359.

Lehr-Lehnardt, R. (2005), 'Non-Governmental Organization Legitimacy: Reassessing Democracy, Accountability, and Transparency', *Cornell Law School LLM Paper Series*, Paper #6, available at: http://lsr.nellco.org/cornell/lps/clacp/6.

Leigh, I. (2004), 'Civil Society, Democracy, and the Law', *Geneva Centre for the Democratic Control of Armed Forces* Working Paper #130 available at: http://www.dcaf.ch/_docs/WP130.pdf.

Lim, C. and Elias, O. (1997), 'The Role of Treaties in the Contemporary International Legal Order', 66 *Nordic J. Intl. L.* 1.

Liotta, P. (2002), 'Boomerang Effect: The Convergence of National and Human Security', 33 *Security Dialogue* 473–488.

Lodgaard, S. (2000), 'Human Security: Concept and Operationalization', availableat:http://www.hsph.%20harvard.edu/hpcr/events/hsworkshop/lodgaard.pdf.

Lord, J. (2004), 'Mirror Mirror on the Wall: Voice Accountability and Non-Governmental Organizations in Human Rights Standard Setting', 5 *Seton Hall J. Diplomacy and Intl. Rel.* 93.

Lynch, R. (1998), 'Is Power All There Is? Michel Foucault and the "Omnipresence" of Power Relations', 42 *Philosophy Today* 65–70.

Major, M. (1992), 'Conscientious Objection and International Law: A Human Right?', 24 *Case Western Reserve Journal of International Law* 349.

Maluwa, T. (1994), 'Custom, Authority and Law: Some Jurisprudential Perspectives on the Theory of Customary International Law', 6 *African J. Intl. L. and Comp. L.* 387.

Marcus, E. (1998), 'Conscientious Objection as an Emerging Human Right', 38 *Virginia Journal of International Law* 507.

Mendelson, M. (2004), 'The effect of customary international law on domestic law: An overview', 4 *Non-State Actors and International Law* 75–85.

Mendelson, M. (1998), 'The Formation of Customary International Law', 272 *Recueil des Cours* 188 at 399.

Merlingen, M. (2003), 'Governmentality: Towards a Foucauldian Framework for the Study of International Governmental Organizations', 38 *Cooperation and Conflict* 361.

Michael, S. (2002), 'The Role of NGOs in Human Security', Hauser Center for Nonprofit Organizations Working Paper No. 12, available at: http://ssrn.com/abstractid=351240.

Mourad, R. (2003), 'After Foucault: A New Form of Right', 29 *Phil. and Social Criticism* 451.

Murphy, M (1999), 'Achieving Economic Security with Swords as Ploughshares: The Modern Use of Force to Combat Environmental Degradation', 39 *Va, J, Intl. L.* 1181.

Murphy, S. (1999), 'Democratic Legitimacy and the Recognition of States', 48 *Intl. and Comp. L. Q.* 545–581.

Newman, D. (2000), 'A Human Security Council? Applying a "Human Security" Agenda to Security Council Reform', 31 *Ottawa L. Rev.* 213.

Newman, S. (2004), 'The Place of Power in Political Discourse', 25 *Intl. Pol. Science Rev.* 139.

Nowrot, K. (1999), 'Legal Consequences of Globalization: The Status of Non-Governmental Organizations Under International Law', 6 *Global Legal Studies J.* 579.

Paris, R. (2001) 'Human Security: Paradigm Shift or Hot Air?', 26 *Intl. Sec.* 87–102.

Park, S. (2004), 'The Role of Transnational Advocacy Networks in Reconstituting International Organisation Identities', 5 *Seton Hall J. Diplomacy and Intl. Rel.* 79.

Pasquino, P. (1993), 'Political Theory of War and Peace: Foucault and the history of modern political theory', 22 *Economy and Society* 77–88.

Peterson, M. (1982), 'Political Use of Recognition: The Influence of the International System', 34 *World Politics* 324.

Prebensen, S. (1998), 'The Margin of Appreciation and Articles 9, 10 and 11 of the Convention', 19 *Human Rights Law Journal* 13.

Rajagopal, B. (2003), 'International Law and Social Movements: Challenges of Theorizing Resistance', 41 *Colum. J. Transnatl. L.* 397.

Raustiala, K. (2002), 'The Architecture of International Cooperation Transgovernmental Networks and the Future of International Law', 43 *Va. J. Intl. L.* 1.

Reinisch, A. and Irgel, C. (2001), 'The participation of non-governmental organizations (NGOs) in the WTO dispute settlement system', 1 *Non-State Actors and International Law* 127.

Roberts, A. (2001), 'Traditional and Modern Approaches to Customary International Law: A Reconciliation', 95 *A. J. Intl. L.* 757.

Rose, N. and Miller, P. (1992), 'Political Power Beyond the State: problematics of government', 43 *British J. Soc.* 173–206.

Salih, M. (2002), 'Islamic NGOs in Africa: The Promise and Peril of Islamic Voluntarism', Centre of African Studies, University of Copenhagen.

Sands, P. (1998) 'Treaty, Custom, and the Cross-fertilization of International Law', 1 *Yale Hum. Rts. Dev. L. J.* 3.

Saskia, H. (1995), 'Mutual Recognition of Croatia and Serbia (+Montenegro)', 6 *E. J. Intl. L.* 598–612.

Saul, B. (2006), 'The Dangers of the United Nations' "New Security Agenda":"Human Security" in the Asia-Pacific Region', 1 *Asian J. Comp. L.* 1.

Saunders, L. (2001), 'Rich and Rare are the Gems they War: Holding De Beers Accountable for Trading Conflict Diamonds', 24 *Fordham Intl. L. J.* 1402.

Scolnicov, A. (2001), 'Children's Right to Freedom of Religion in a Multi-Religious Society', *Centre for Studies on New Religions.*

Scott, G. and Carr, C. (1996), 'Multilateral Treaties and the Formation of Customary International Law', 25 *Denv. J. Intl. L. & Pol.* 71.

Seidensticker, E. (2002), 'Human Security, Human Rights and Human Development', available at: http://www.humansecurity-chs.org/activities/outreach/0206harvard.pdf.

Shoham, U. (1996), 'The Principle of Legality and the Israeli Military Government in the Territories', 153 *Mil. L. Rev.* 245.

Siegel, R. (1992), 'Reasoning from the Body: A Historical Perspective on Abortion Regulation and Questions of Equal Protection', 44 *Stanford Law Review* 261.

Simpson, G. (2000), 'The Situation on the International Legal Theory Front: The Power of Rules and the Rule of Power', 11 *Eur. J. Intl L.* 439.

Slimm, H. (2002), 'By What Authority? The Legitimacy and Accountability of Non-Governmental Organizations', *Journal of Humanitarian Assistance* available at: www.jha.ac/articles/a082htm.

Sloane, R. (2002), 'The Changing Face of Recognition in International Law: A Case Study of Tibet', 16 *Emory Intl. L. Rev.* 107.

Smith, S. (2001), 'Globalization and the Governance of Space: a critique of Krasner on Sovereignty', 1 *Intl. Rel. of the Asia Pacific* 199.

Stark, B. (2002), 'After/word(s): "Violations of Human Dignity" and Postmodern International Law', 27 *Yale J. Intl. L.* 315.

Strenski, I. (1998), 'Religion, Power, and Final Foucault', 66 *J. American Academy of Rel.* 345.

Suhrke, A. (1999), 'Human Security and the Interests of States', 30 *Security Dialogue* 265–276.

Tadros, V. (1998), 'Between Governance and Discipline: The Law and Michel Foucault', 18 *Oxford Journal of Legal Studies* 75.

Thomas, N. and Tow, E. (2002), 'The Utility of Human Security: Sovereignty and Humanitarian Intervention', 33 *Security Dialogue* 177–192.

Thomson, J. (1995), 'State Sovereignty in International Relations: Bridging the Gap Between Theory and Empirical Research', 39 *Intl. Studies Q.* 213.

Tinker, C. (1992), '"Environmental Security" in the United Nations: Not a Matter for the Security Council', 59 *Tenn. L. Rev.* 787.

Vagts, D. (2004), 'International Relations Looks at Customary International Law: A Traditionalist's Defence', 15 *E. J. Intl. L. 1031.*

Walden, R. (1977), 'The Subjective Element in the Formation of Customary International Law', 12 *Is. L. Rev.* 344.

Walden, R. (1978), 'Customary International Law: A Jurisprudential Analysis', 13 *Is. L. Rev.* 86.

Walzer, M. (2001), 'Universalism and Jewish Values', transcript of 15/5/01 speech, available at: http://www.cceia.org/viewMedia.php/prmID/114.

Warkentin, C.and Mingst, K. (2000), 'International Institutions, the State, and Global Civil Society in the Age of the World Wide Web', 6 *Global Governance* 237–257.

Watkin, K. (2004), 'Controlling the Use of Force: A Role for Human Rights Norms in Contemporary Armed Conflict', 98 *Am. J. Intl. L.* 1–34.

Wolf, A. (1999), 'Water and Human Security', 3 *AVISO: An Information Bulletin on Global Environmental Change and Human Security*, available at: http://www.peacemagazine.org/9910/wurfel.htm.

Index

AIDS 119

belief, freedom of *see* freedom of religion or belief
bio-politics, Foucault 111

China (Beijing) 37, 38
China (Taiwan), recognition 37–8
Civil and Political Rights, International Covenant 75
coercion, international human rights as 72
commemoration case, social discourse 88, 92
communitarian approach, human rights 130
consensual approach, vs normative approach 10
corporations, and human rights 132
customary international law
- constituents 63
- and customary norms 56, 60, 66, 67
- as dialogue 62
- discourse formation 63, 63–4
- domestic law, status 51
- external aspects 57–8, 67
- formation 50, 51, 62
- internal aspects 52–7
- international organizations 57–8
- non-state actors 57, 58, 67
- as ongoing discourse 63, 67
- *opinio juris* 51, 52, 53, 54, 58, 59, 60, 61, 65
- problems 52–9
- realist views 62
- on sliding scale 56–7
- as source of international law 4, 49–50, 51, 59
- and state practice 53–5, 58, 60, 65
- subjective elements 53
- transformative approach 68–9
- transgressive approach 61, 62
- treaties, relationship 130

customary norms 4
- and customary international law 56, 60, 66, 67
- sources 68

democracy, extension of, and global civil society 119
disciplinary mechanism, power as 25
disciplinary mechanisms, Foucault on 24, 47
discourse
- Foucault on 64
- ongoing
- individual beliefs as 85, 89
- truth as 84

discourse formation 1, 4, 21–2, 63, 64, 126
- customary international law 63–4
- freedom of religion or belief 91
- function 22
- individual beliefs 83–4
- knowledge from 22, 64, 65
- state as 3, 90

environment, and human security 99
epistemology, Foucault on 82
- *see also* knowledge

Falun-Gong cult 76
Foucault, Michel
- approaches 1–2, 3, 129, 132, 133
- bio-politics 111

on disciplinary mechanisms 24, 47
on discourse 64
on epistemology 82
on governmentality 61, 112
on knowledge 26–7, 84
on law 20
on power 3, 19, 22–3, 24, 26, 27, 42, 44, 90, 131
on the state 3, 90
on thought 83
transgressive approach 3, 18, 79, 88
freedom of religion or belief 5, 73–80
bias towards recognized religions 76–7
commemoration case 88
definition problems 74–5, 76
discourse formation 91
headscarf case 94
and minority beliefs 93
obstacles 73–4, 75–6
ritual slaughter case 86–8
social process 78–80
transgressive approach 83, 90
see also individual beliefs

Geneva Convention 105
global civil society 6, 116, 124
emergence 117
and extension of democracy 119
goals 119
influence 125
meaning 117
and non-governmental organizations 120
non-state actors 119, 128
post-cold War 118
and power 126–7
role 117–18
and the state 123
global cultural models, and states 15
globalization 9, 12, 16, 45, 118, 132
and the social economy 98
governmentality, Foucault on 61, 112

headscarf case 94
human rights
communitarian approach 130
and corporations 132
and human security 101–2, 115
and the state 106
transgressive approach 115–16
Universal Declaration 74, 75
see also international human rights
Human Rights, European Convention 86
Human Rights, European Court 76, 94
Human Rights Council, UN 131
human security 5
alternative approach 109–12
and the environment 99
goals 99–100
and human rights 101–2, 115
institutional protection 109
integrative concept 98, 99
and international law 98
and liberty 110
multilateral structure 110
non-state actors 108–9, 110, 111, 115
non-territoriality 109
outer limits, exploration 130
and power 112
as process 110
scope 100–2, 104, 106–7
and the state 103, 107–8, 110–11, 113
traditional approaches 100
transactionalism 110–11, 113
transformative approach 111–12
UN Commission on 98

individual beliefs
as contingent ideas 86

discourse formation 83–4
formation 80–1
manifestation 81
as ongoing discourse 85, 89
as search for truth 92
as search for understanding 85
social factors 81, 95
transformative approach 84
transgressive approach 93
individual liberty, and state sovereignty 91
institutional protection, human security 109
International Court of Justice 132
International Criminal Court 132
international human rights 5
as coercion 72
forum internum, *forum externum*, distinction 81
non-Western approaches 130
perspectives 72
problems 71
and recognition of states 36, 38–9, 45
and shared sovereignty 104
transformative approach 72
see also freedom of religion or belief; human security
international law
ambiguity 10
compliance-based theory 14, 16
constituents 4
constructive approach 15
current interpretations 2
customary international law, as source 4, 49–50, 51, 59
enforcement problems 9
fluidity 16
and human security 98
and international legal theory 28
and international organizations 2, 8, 57
and international relations 8, 13, 14
interpretations 2, 8
and lack of legal system 9–10
as law 8
legitimacy doctrine 7, 13, 14
and natural law 11
and non-governmental organizations 121
and non-state actors 3, 6, 16, 17, 19, 24, 28
normative approach 10–11, 12, 13, 16
structure 2
objective standards 10–11
positivist view 11
and power 18–19, 131
realist views 8–9, 11, 12, 16
as reflection of state interests 12
and social movements 17–18
sociological models 13–14, 15
sources 4, 10, 49
state role 10, 11, 16, 18–19
state-centric model 2, 12
and transgovernmentalism 16
transgressive approach 19
universalist views 8
see also customary international law
international legal theory 3
and international law 28
and the international system 10
international organizations
customary international law 57–8
and international law 2, 8, 57
states, effects on 15
international recognition *see* recognition of states
international relations, and international law 8, 13, 14
international society, transgressive approach 9
international system 6
complexity 129
and international legal theory 10
non-state actors 22, 27, 28

and recognition of states 33, 41
tensions within 15
transformative approach 9
transgressive approach 17

knowledge
derivation 85–6
development 44
Foucault on 26–7, 84
from discourse formation 22, 64, 65
and power 3, 25–7, 46, 95
role 26, 46
as social condition 82
as truth 84

language 83
law
disciplinary role 20, 21
Foucault on 20
international law as 8
productive role 20, 21
Law of the Sea Tribunal 58
legitimacy doctrine, international law 7, 13, 14
liberty, and human security 110

migrant workers 131
minority beliefs 93
moral standards, formation 81

natural law, and international law 11
neo-liberalism 17
non-governmental organizations 4, 5, 6
accountability 116–17
fluidity 127
and global civil society 120
influence 121
internal differences 124
and international law 121
normative legitimacy 121–3
and power 127–8
problems 121–4, 128
non-state actors
customary international law 57, 58, 67
global civil society 119, 128
human security 108–9, 110, 111, 115
and international law 3, 6, 16, 17, 19, 24, 28, 57
international system 22, 27, 28
and power 25
normative approach
international law 10–11, 12, 13, 16
meaning 10
vs consensual approach 10

opinio juris
criticism of 55–7
customary international law 51, 52, 53, 54, 58, 59, 60, 61, 65
meaning 55
transformative effects 65

positivist view, international law 11
power
as disciplinary mechanism 25, 46, 47
dispersal of 24–5, 95
distributive function 25, 46
fluidity 19, 23–4, 27, 42
Foucault on 3, 19, 22–3, 24, 26, 27, 42, 44, 90, 131
and global civil society 126–7
and human security 112
and international law 18–19, 131
and knowledge 3, 25–7, 46, 95
and non-governmental organizations 127–8
and non-state actors 25
and recognition of states 41
resistance to 24, 47
and rights claims 25
and social actors 18, 23, 24
and social change 92

and social forces 47
and social identities 20
as subjective notion 23
transformative approach to 128
as transgressive notion 22, 27, 46, 47
power relations 23–4
privatization 18, 108, 118, 127
process, and recognition of states 33–9

realist views
customary international law 62
international law 8–9, 11, 12, 16
recognition of states
alternative 39–47
China (Taiwan) 37–8
constitutive 31, 32, 34, 36, 45
construct role 40
declarative 31, 33, 34, 39
effects 30, 38–40
facilitative role 34, 35, 37, 38, 43, 45
fluidity 40–1, 48
further research 130
and human rights 36, 38–9, 45
instrumental 34, 35–6, 37, 38, 40, 45
and the international system 33, 41
normative 39, 42
and power 41
and process 33–9, 130
social factors 39–40
and statehood 29–33, 39
transformative approach 30, 41, 42–7, 48
transgressive approach 130
religion
development 91–2
freedom of *see* freedom of religion or belief
role in states 77–8
social function 79
and social process 81–3
rights claims, and power 25
see also human rights; international human rights
Rights of Indigenous Peoples, Declaration 131
ritual slaughter case 86–8
social discourse 87, 92

Scientology 76
social actors, and power 18, 23, 24
social change, and power 92
social condition, knowledge as 82
social discourse
commemoration case 88
ritual slaughter case 87, 92
social economy, and globalization 98
social factors, individual beliefs 81, 95
social forces, and power 47
social identities, and power 20
social movements
and international law 17–18
vs state-centric model 18
social process, and religion 81–3
social product, state sovereignty as 19
social relations 5, 28, 44, 45
transgressive approach 88–9
sociological models
international law 13–14, 15
sovereignty 15
sovereignty
shared, and international human rights 104
sociological models 15
see also state sovereignty
state
as discourse formation 3, 90
Foucault on 3, 90
and global civil society 123
and human rights 106
and human security 103, 107–8, 110–11, 113

territoriality 109
transformative approach to 112–13
state practice, and customary international law 53–5, 58, 60, 65
state role, international law 10, 11, 16, 18–19
state sovereignty
and individual liberty 91
as social product 19
sociological models 15
state-centric model
international law 2
vs social movements 18
statehood, and recognition 29–33, 39
states
declarations 55–6
effects of international organizations 15
and global cultural models 15
role of religion 77–8

thought, Foucault on 83
transactionalism, human security 110–11, 113
transformative approach
customary international law 68–9
human security 111–12
individual beliefs 84
international human rights 72
international system 9
recognition of states 30, 41, 42–7, 48
to power 128
to the state 112–13
transgovernmentalism, and international law 16
transgressive approach
customary international law 61, 62
Foucault 3, 18, 79, 88
freedom of religion or belief 83, 90
human rights 115–16
individual beliefs 93
international law 19
international system 17
recognition of states 130
social relations 88–9
to international society 9
transgressive notion, power as 22, 27, 46, 47
treaties 49
customary international law, relationship 130
truth
individual beliefs as search for 92
knowledge as 84
as ongoing discourse 84

Women, Discrimination Against, Convention 73
World Trade Organisation (WTO) 33–4, 58, 120